THE ONLY
GAME IN TOWN

THE ONLY
GAME IN TOWN

An Illustrated History of Gambling

by Hank Messick and Burt Goldblatt

THOMAS Y. CROWELL COMPANY

Established 1834

New York

Designed by Burt Goldblatt

Manufactured in the United States of America
Library of Congress Cataloging in Publication Data

Messick, Hank.
  The only game in town.

  Includes index.
  1. Gambling—United States—History. I. Goldblatt, Burt, joint author. II. Title.
HV6715.M48 1976   301.5'7   75-26583
ISBN 0-690-01061-3

1 2 3 4 5 6 7 8 9 10

For Marda,
A hardway bettor
and for Margo,
who played a long shot

Books by Hank Messick and Burt Goldblatt:

The Mobs and the Mafia
Gangs and Gangsters
Kidnapping
The Only Game in Town

CONTENTS

Doubtless the pleasure is as great
Of being cheated as to cheat.
    Samuel Butler

A wise gamester ought to take the dice
Even as they fall, and pay down quietly
Rather than grumble at his luck.
      Sophocles

INTRODUCTION

There's a school of thought which holds that Eve ate the apple to settle a bet; she had a small wager with the serpent as to the number of seeds it contained.

She swallowed one of the seeds and so lost the bet. In addition, she became pregnant.

The belief that the impulse to gamble is as old as woman and as powerful as the sex drive has been around a long time and perhaps has more converts today than ever, since it offers a quick-healing salve for the fever blisters of the soul.

George Devol, who wrote the classic *Forty Years a Gambler on the Mississippi,* tells of the time when love came face to face with the gambling instinct. He was still a young man, just getting started as a riverboat sharpie, when one night on the steamer *Magnolia* he met a "fascinating" young widow. He danced with her all evening, neglecting his livelihood, and next day was rewarded with an invitation to visit her plantation. "After three days of happiness," he wrote, "I tore myself away, feeling as if I was 'unfixed for life.'" They met again on another steamer and this time she gave him a diamond ring to wear "until we meet again." He bade her good-bye at the stage-plank and sailed away so depressed it was an hour or more before "I started out to find a sucker." The memory of the beautiful widow haunted him. "I have often thought," he wrote, "what a different man I might have been."

Perhaps one reason that love and sex take second place to gambling is the tradition that gambling, somehow, in and of itself, is an expression of virility. This theory doesn't account, of course, for the millions of women gamblers, and it runs counter to the views of some psychologists who hold that gambling is really a sex substitute for men who are trying to find a way of losing with grace. Nevertheless, the view persists, as is illustrated by this statement of a few years back in *The Catholic Digest:* "Risk is rightly thrilling, fate is fascinating, and luck is luring. It may not be possible to discern all the emotions involved: the bravery and the fear, the hope and the dread, the greed and the prodigality. But in their best mixture they are powerful and exhilarating; they give life its zest, effort its spur, *and man his masculinity.* The timid man seldom forges ahead, and the one who fears to gamble will never have the thrill of a win. He may console himself that he will never lose either, but he probably has little to lose, and worry will kill what fun he gets from hoarding what he has." (Italics added.)

The late "Trigger Mike" Coppola, who forged far ahead by killing people and taking the

Adam and Eve about to eat the forbidden fruit, taking the first gamble with life.

gamble out of the numbers racket, enjoyed an occasional fling at the crap tables in Las Vegas. When he won, he gave his wife a fraction of the loot; when he lost, he beat her savagely. If the latter was an expression of masculinity, Ann Coppola would have settled for a more conventional gesture. But Mike, she reported, was a poor bed partner.

Yet there's no question that gambling and sex were associated in the beginning. Ask the Egyptians. As they tell it, Rhea (Earth) was having a clandestine affair with Saturn and became pregnant. Outraged, the Sun ruled that she couldn't be delivered of her child during any month or year. To the rescue came Mercury, who was also in love with Rhea. He gambled with the Moon "at tables" and won from that goddess one-seventieth of her light. Out of this he fashioned five new days, and Rhea used them to give birth to Isis and Osiris. Eventually, the five new days were added to the 360 then in use, and were observed by the Egyptians for centuries as the birthdays of their gods.

Regular dice of ivory, known as "Astragals," have been found in the ancient temples of Egypt, so it seems safe to assume that Mercury used dice in his out-of-this-world duel with the Moon.

Gods, gambling, and sex got mixed up together because sex was part of the process of creation, a process the gods controlled, and games of chance were considered about the only way to learn the will of the gods in any given situation.

The Bible gives many examples of executive buck-passing by means of "lots." Moses, for example, cast lots to divide the land of Canaan among the people of Israel, but he credited the Lord with the inspiration. Presumably, if someone was unhappy with Moses's rocky subdivision, he could blame the Lord and not Moses. Aaron said he was commanded by the Lord to cast lots to determine which of two goats went to the Lord and which became "the scapegoat." And when Jonah tried to duck a preaching assignment, along with some colleagues, he was chosen by lot to get swallowed by the whale.

One wonders how the ancients would have explained George Devol's adventure on the riverboat *Princess*. Leaving Baton Rouge one Sunday morning, Devol began playing roulette in the boat's barbershop. Thirty-five gamblers crowded in and he was doing "a land-office business" when suddenly the boat blew up. Not one of the gamblers was

This scene, recorded on a marble plaque at Pompeii, shows a group of women playing knucklebones, a game inherited from the Greeks.

A page from the Koran, the book which contains the Moslems' theology, moral code, and religious ordinances—and classifies gambling as a sin.

hurt, but fourteen preachers, en route to New Orleans to attend a convention, were among the one hundred souls "who landed into eternity without a moment's warning."

So convinced were the ancient Jews that gambling was a form of divine revelation that they tried to punish all who used it for mercenary purposes. Disqualified from serving as a judge or witness were "the dice-player, the lender of money on interest, the flyer of doves who wagers on the race." Moreover, the Jew who won silver or something of value from another Jew by means of gambling was guilty of theft. If, however, he won it from a gentile, that was no crime.

The Moslems, coming along later, classed wine and gambling together. The Koran states flatly that "in both there is great sin, and also some things of use unto men, but their sinfulness is greater than their use." Needless to say, given such a loophole as that, the Moslems were great gamblers as well as great drinkers.

It would seem that man's itch to gamble has always been rewarded with loopholes in the laws of God and certainly in the laws he draws for himself. The Greeks considered gambling a great sin, but there was so much of it that Aristotle noted that "thieves and robbers at least took great risks for their spoils while gamblers gained from their friends to whom they ought rather to give." The Romans had severe laws against gambling in the early eons, but even they relaxed their rules during the annual December orgy they called the Saturnalia. In later, more decadent days, gambling was widespread and wide open. Loaded dice and gaming tables were found beneath the

Card players de-
picted in a fifteenth-
century tapestry.

5

ashes that fell on Pompeii, proving that things then were much as they are now.

Actually, then, it isn't necessary to study the relics of the past to understand that as civilizations evolved, as wealth piled up unevenly, as men became frustrated and bored, gambling promised excitement and offered the illusion of hope. Despite a few thousand years of ideals and lip service to moral laws, man has changed so little that we can reverse the usual process and comprehend his past by studying his present. The street festivals in New York, for example, in honor of various saints, make great use of the gambling urge, and the illegality of some of the church-sponsored fun and games is blandly ignored by police despite the participation of known underworld figures. We continue to make folk heroes out of such characters as "Nick the Greek," publicizing his occasional correct estimates of the odds and ignoring his many failures. Steadfastly, we refuse to learn by experience. No need to wonder, then, why man continues to throw good money after bad. We need only turn to a friend of George Devol, one "Canada Bill" Jones. Marooned one night in a river town, Jones went looking for some "action." He found it in the backroom of the barbershop. Warned that the play was crooked, Bill replied:

"I know, but it's the only game in town."

The swindler Canada Bill trimming a sucker at three-card monte, his specialty. Canada Bill operated in California and throughout the Northwest, but when he tried operating on trains, the Pinkerton men sent him running.

1 SINCE TIME BEGAN

Things haven't changed very much since Samson tried to pull a fast one.

The son of Manoah was fully grown but hardly knew his strength when among the Philistines he spotted a woman who pleased him well.

En route to visit her he met a young lion who roared against him. With some help from the Lord, Samson tore the lion apart and went on to talk to the woman.

After returning home, Samson began thinking about the woman and decided he would take her for a wife. Once more he went to Timnath where the woman lived. Stopping by the carcass of the lion, he discovered that a swarm of bees had settled therein and made much honey. The meat was good, too.

And Samson, no great thinker, had an idea.

At the wedding feast he told his thirty guests that he had a riddle to ask, and he bet them thirty changes of garments that they could not solve it within seven days. The riddle:

Out of the eater came forth meat
And out of the strong came forth sweetness.

Since Samson had told no one of the lion the guests were puzzled, and after three days they began to sweat a little. Going to the young wife, they ordered her to "entice thy husband" and learn the answer to the riddle.

If she didn't, they threatened, they would burn down her father's house.

The wife proceeded to weep for the next four days until Samson, tired of her tears, told her the solution. She passed it along, and on the seventh day the men beat the deadline with this answer:

What is sweeter than honey?
And what is stronger than a lion?

Samson replied:

If ye had not plowed with my heifer
Ye had not found out my riddle.

Even so, he felt obliged to pay off the bet. And, like a lot of men since, he had bet without possessing the means of paying off. So he went out on the street, so to speak, in this case to Ashkelon, murdered thirty men and robbed them of their clothes. Then he paid off the bet.

The Lord's work went on. When Christ was crucified, Roman soldiers gambled for His rags as He hung on the Cross. Centuries passed and, in time, Richard I of England and Philip of France led an army on the first crusade. Before the army could move, however, the two kings thought it necessary to issue an edict regulating gambling. All

Above, Samson, one
of the early
bettors—and losers.
Below, Roman sol-
diers gambling for
the clothes of Jesus
while he is being cru-
cified.

persons in the army beneath the rank of knight were forbidden to gamble for money. Knights, clergymen, and attendants of the kings were permitted to play for money but could lose no more than twenty shillings in twenty-four hours. The two kings, of course, could play for whatever sum they pleased. Persons violating this law were to be stripped and whipped through the army for three days in a row.

In 1650, Nick L'Estrange of Hunstanton, England, wrote a book about gambling, which today is in the British Museum. Typical of the stories it contains is one about Sir William Herbert's dice. It seems that Sir William was dicing with a friend and disagreed with him over a cast. The friend insisted he had thrown a 4 and a 5. Sir William swore mightily and said:

"Thou art a perjured knave; for, give me a sixpence, and if there be a four upon the dice, I will return you a thousand pounds."

He won the sixpence, for he had been using crooked dice "of a high cut"—that is, without a four. The moral might be: "Don't try to cheat a cheater." But morals don't always apply, as witness the case of the Chevalier d'Eon.

It began when a surgeon named Hayes bet a broker named Jacques in 1771 that the distinquished diplomat from France, the Chevalier d'Eon, was in reality a woman instead of the man he professed to be. Jacques promised to pay one hundred guineas for every guinea Dr. Hayes put up when d'Eon was proved a woman. Six years later, the doctor had put up seven hundred guineas and he went into court to collect his winnings. The Lord Chief Justice presided.

Richard, Coeur de Lion, triumphant at the battle at Acre during the Crusades, regulated gambling among his troops.

Dr. Hayes presented as witness another surgeon who testified he had treated the Chevalier d'Eon from the time that individual had been appointed ambassador to England. His professional services had been such, the doctor explained, that he knew for a fact that d'Eon was a woman. This testimony was confirmed by another reputable witness who swore the Chevalier had displayed a female bosom to him and a female wardrobe as well.

Jacques, overwhelmed by this evidence, made no attempt to prove that d'Eon was a man. Instead, he claimed that Dr. Hayes by virtue of his superior knowledge had taken advantage of him in making a wager and the bet should be declared invalid. Moreover, such an indecent case should never have come before the court in the first place.

Lord Mansfeld, the chief justice, agreed the trial had been indecent but he insisted it was the unnecessary questions put by the defense that made it so. It was enough for the witnesses to swear d'Eon was a woman; they should not have been asked how they acquired their knowledge. But since all the facts had indicated d'Eon was a man, and the truth about her sex might not have become known except for some accidents, the wager was valid and the only question to be decided was the winner. The Lord Chief Justice recommended the jury find for Dr. Hayes.

The jury did find for Hayes, but only to the extent of ruling he could recover the seven hundred guineas he had bet in the first place. In effect, the jury canceled the wager.

It proved to be a wise verdict if not a just one. Thirty-three years later the individual legally judged to be a woman died in London. Examination proved conclusively that the Chevalier d'Eon was a man.

When gambling in merry old England reached the state where women became addicted, there were new problems for the hapless male. Consider this lament in *The Guardian* of July 29, 1713:

"My friend, *Theophrastus,* the best of Husbands and of Fathers, has often com-

On the left, William Crockford, and above, a scene at the gaming tables in his plush gambling club in London.

plained to me with Tears in his Eyes of the late Hours he is forced to keep if he would enjoy his wife's Conversation. When she returns to me with Joy in her Face, it does not arise, says he, from the Sight of her Husband, but from the Good Luck she has had at cards. On the contrary, says he, if she has been a Loser, I am doubly a Sufferer by it. She comes home out of humour, is angry with every Body, displeased with all I can do, or say, and, in Reality, for no other reason but because she has been throwing away my Estate.''

The writer went on to complain that a night of gambling ruins a woman's looks. ''I never knew a thorough paced Female Gamester hold her Beauty two winters together.'' But there was another problem as well, and he spelled it out quite plainly:

''All Play debts must be paid in Specie, or by an Equivalent. The Man who plays beyond his Income, pawns his Estate; the Woman must find something else to Mortgage when her Pin Money is gone. The Husband has his Lands to dispose of, the Wife her Person.''

Of course, if she had lost her looks from too much gaming, her ''Person'' might not have been worth very much.

But complaints of sore losers aside, men and women continued to gamble, and opportunity offered itself to a fishmonger's son, one William Crockford. Becoming a skilled hand at whist, piquet, and cribbage, as well as a bookmaker, Crockford founded the famous gambling house that bore his name. A contemporary description makes it plain that Crockford's was lavish enough to have made Bugsy Siegel, of Las Vegas fame, jaundiced:

George Washington was a frequent
visitor to the Williamsburg Jockey
Club, particularly during race week.
An entry in his diary for 1772
mentions that he lost £1/6 in bets at
Annapolis. During his New York
campaign he acquired a white
oriental stallion, Lindsey's Arabian,
whose blood persists in
thoroughbred pedigrees to this day.

"On entering from the street, a magnificent
vestibule and staircase breaks upon the
view; to the right and left of the hall are
reading and dining rooms. The staircase is of
a sinuous form, sustained in its landing by
four columns of the Doric order, above
which are a series of examples of the Ionic
order, forming a quadrangle with apertures
to the chief apartments. Above the pillars is a
covered ceiling, perforated with luminous
panels of stained glass, from which springs
a dome of surpassing beauty: from the dome
depends a lantern containing a magnificent
chandelier."

And that was just the beginning. The state
drawing room was described as "baffling
perfect description of its beauty, but
decorated in the most florid style of Louis
Quatorze." And the upholstery and other
decorations were said to be "imitative of the
gorgeous taste of George the Fourth."

Perhaps, but George IV didn't approve. The
Times of London on January 1, 1828, carried
a discreet little story describing how "the
monarch . . . in his usual nervous style,
denounced such infamous receptacles for
plunder as not only a disgrace to the country
at large but the age in which we live." The
headline above the story was: CROCKFORD'S
HELL. But if the king was critical, England
was not. Statesmen, authors, soldiers, and
poets were proud to be members, and
visitors such as Prince Talleyrand belonged.
The son of the fishmonger was one of the
richest men in England when he died in
1844.

Europe exported gamblers and antigambling
sentiment in almost equal measure to
America, so, when their ships landed, the
colonists were variously amused and shocked
to find the Indians already gambling. Dice
made from pear and plum pits were popular,
and there was sports betting as well—betting
on games of skill similar to football. The
noble redskin not only took to the white
man's liquor, but went wild over his
playing cards. The Puritans of New England

Left, Thomas Jefferson is said to be
the only future president of the
United States to oppose an
incumbent president at the
racetrack. Magnolia, one of the first
foals sired by Lindsey's Arabian for
Washington, was defeated in an
Alexandria Jockey Club race by a
colt owned by Jefferson. Above,
General "Light Horse Harry" Lee
purchased Magnolia from George
Washington in 1788 for 5,000 acres
of Kentucky land.

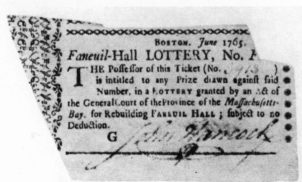

made it illegal to bring cards into the colony, but still they came. Lotteries came into official use when the Virginia Company was authorized to conduct one in 1612 to finance its colony at Jamestown. Within a hundred years, private lotteries were fashionable. Brick houses were often given as prizes, and the tickets were expensive enough to be worthy of men who could afford such dwellings.

Thomas Jefferson regarded the lottery as ''a salutary instrument'' for disposing of property so valuable that no single purchaser could be found. Jefferson also enjoyed gambling, and in the three weeks from June 10 to July 2, 1776, when he was drafting the Declaration of Independence, he relaxed at backgammon, lotto, and other gambling games. His records show he lost heavily. In 1826, eighty-three years old and heavily burdened with debts—gambling and other-wise—he petitioned Virginia for permission to dispose of his property by means of a lottery or, as he put it: "To sell it in a way which will offend no moral principle, and expose none to risk but the willing, and those wishing to be permitted to take the chance of gain.''

Permission was granted, but he died before the lottery could be held and his debts paid.

George Washington also sought to use the lottery for his own purposes. In 1768 he sponsored a lottery to construct a road across the Blue Ridge to an area famous for hot springs in what was then Augusta County. Why did Washington want to make that region more easily reached? His step-daughter, Patsy Curtis, suffered from epilepsy, and it was believed that bathing in the springs might cure her.

Examples of early lottery tickets. Top to bottom: dated 1762, this lottery ticket was purchased to aid in the rebuilding of Faneuil Hall in Boston; signed by George Washington in 1768, this ticket has become highly prized by collectors; another lottery for the rebuilding of Faneuil Hall, dated 1765 and signed by John Hancock. Also, a lottery wheel dating from 1830; note the child drawing the ticket.

A Declaration for the certaine time of drawing the great standing Lottery.

VVelcomes.

To him that first shall bee drawne out with a Blanke — 100. Crownes
To the second — 50. Crownes
To the third — 25. Crownes
To him that every day during the drawing of this Lottery shall bee first drawne out with a Blanke — 10. Crownes

Prizes.

1. Great Prize of — 4500. Crownes
2. Great Prizes, each of — 2000. Crownes
4. Great Prizes, each of — 1000. Crownes
6. Great Prizes, each of — 500. Crownes
10. Prizes each of — 300. Crownes
20. Prizes, each of — 200. Crownes
100. Prizes, each of — 100. Crownes

An early lottery broadside from the Virginia lottery issued in 1615 to raise funds for the Virginia Company. Below, the Spanish milled dollar Washington awarded to the winners of the athletic competitions he instigated in an attempt to discourage gambling among his troops. When change was needed it was sometimes cut up into bits — four bits equalled a half-dollar and two bits a quarter, thus the expressions still heard today.

Tickets bearing Washington's signature were printed and are a collector's item today, but few were sold and no drawing was held. Patsy died in 1773, and the road across the mountains was abandoned. But so-called curative springs have a strange affinity for gamblers, and in time White Sulphur Springs developed a huge resort named Greenbrier. Wealthy arthritics could gamble between baths at the Clover Club, a small but exquisite casino when the author visited it a few years ago. Strictly illegal, of course, but anyone who flashed a hundred-dollar bill in the dining room could get inside without difficulty. Late in the 1940s the Cleveland syndicate considered building a major casino there and took option on some land, but it dropped the project in favor of the Desert Inn in Las Vegas.

With the coming of the Revolution, Washington and his colleagues sought to encourage a new morality as part of the national purpose. The First Continental Congress in 1774 adopted a resolution to "discountenance and discourage every species of extravagance and dissipation, especially all horse-racing and all kinds of gaming. . . ." The attempt was unsuccessful, of course, and in 1776 Washington issued a general order to his army:

"All officers, non-commissioned officers, and soldiers, are positively forbid playing at cards, or other games of chance. At this time of public distress, men may find enough to do, in the service of their God and their country, without abandoning themselves to vice and immorality."

General Washington arranged for footraces, wrestling matches, and the like, offering prizes to the winner in an effort to curb the appetite for gambling. Some of the men cherished the Spanish milled dollar personally presented by Washington for athletic excellence, but most of the soldiers considered it too little reward for too much exertion. It was easier to watch—and bet with their fellows on the outcome. The war on gambling was one of Washington's less successful campaigns.

British troops had their problems as well but, less concerned with winning divine favor—they had the king on their side—than the rebels, they didn't worry about it as much. In addition to the usual games of chance, they brought along faro and introduced it to the wealthy citizens of New York. It proved to be an intriguing, if expensive, way of passing the dull winters.

Faro was no newcomer to America. Thanks to an exiled Scotsman named John Law, it had become quite the rage in New Orleans early in the century. Law was an adventurer and something of a genius as well. His career began in 1694 when, at the age of twenty-three, he killed Edward "Beau" Wilson in a duel at London. The fight was fair, but Wilson had connections; Law fled to the Continent where he became known as the "king of gamblers." After winning in Brussels and Vienna, he went to Paris in 1708 and set up a faro game at the home of an actress. In short order he won 67,000 pounds sterling, and French police threw him out of the country.

Faro was a card game invented by the French, who adapted it from the Venetian game of *basetta*. It got its name from the fact that early French cards bore a picture of an Egyptian pharaoh on the back. It was a "bank game," meaning the players were pitted against the house instead of each other. When played "on the square," the percentage favored the house, but by a margin so small as to be unimportant. This encouraged the suckers who perhaps didn't understand that the opportunities for cheating were greater than in almost any other game. A clever banker could win immense sums very quickly with faro.

Faro enjoyed considerable popularity before being prohibited by Louis XIV. By the time John Law appeared, however, the king was in ill health and his wishes were no longer enforced so strictly. Following the death of the king in 1715, the Duke of Orleans became regent, and John Law returned to France. He had used his leisure time to study banking and was convinced he had found a way to wealth that surpassed even faro. Nevertheless, the gambling game became popular

Opposite page, top, financial genius John Law of Lauriston, also called "King of the Gamblers." Below, a Dutch cartoon of 1720 ridiculing John Law and his bubble scheme, showing the night share crier and his magic lantern. Above, another Dutch caricature of Law, crowned by folly.

The fall of Law's financial empire. Note on the left, a ruined investor jumping from a window, a foreshadowing of what happened in Wall Street in 1929. Opposite page, Louis XIV of France who banned faro during his reign.

again, and the inclination to gamble was stimulated when the regent accepted Law's theories on credit and paper money.

In short order, the ex-gambler became the head of *Banque Royale,* able to issue paper money guaranteed by the regent, and obtained trade and colonization rights to that vast territory in America known as Louisiana. Law launched a gigantic promotion, assuring Frenchmen that the country across the ocean was full of gold and gems and lovely Indian maids. Tens of thousands invested and sailed for America before the "Mississippi bubble," as it came to be known, burst. Law had to leave France in a hurry once more, and his vast estates were confiscated.

The czar asked him to take care of Russia's finances, but the challenge was too much. Faro was safer. Law settled in Italy where he continued to gamble until his death in 1729. Meanwhile, thousands of Frenchmen made New Orleans a model of Paris and faro spread up river and along the coast as more and more professionals saw the opportunities for cheating the unwary.

The same money-hungry Frenchmen brought along with them another card game known as *poque.* It was modified somewhat when some Yankee sailors introduced a Persian game called *As Nas,* which offered more

combinations to bet upon, but the French still called it *poque.* Later, of course, after traders began dropping down the river from British-held lands, the name changed first to *poke* and then to *poker,* in the same language change in which French ten-dollar notes became known as *dixies* and New Orleans as "dixieland."

When Louisiana was bought by the United States, the French influence spread more rapidly. And so did gambling. Before the advent of steam, traffic by water was largely one-way—down the river. The pioneers from upcountry sent down their furs, their skins, their corn, and their corn liquor by flatboat. With the money they got in New Orleans, they bought slaves, clothes, and glass for their windows. Such goods had to be carried overland, of course, so highwaymen and gamblers flourished. Conditions became so bad that preachers began warning of hellfire and the world's end. On December 16, 1811, an earthquake shook the Mississippi and many thought the preachers had called the turn—to use a phrase associated with faro. As houses collapsed and men dropped to their knees, some gamblers kept right on playing. Told the end was imminent, one gambler in Paducah glanced upward at heaven and implored, "Let me finish this hand, please Lord."

By coincidence, the earthquake—actually it was a series of quakes over a three-month period—which caused the waters of the Mississippi to run backward, occurred the same year that Robert Fulton's first "swimming volcano" chugged downriver from Pittsburgh. The preachers may have considered steamboats the final indignity to arouse God's wrath—certainly they brought a great increase in commerce and thus a corresponding increase in villainy. For now boats could go upstream as well as down. The first to do so was the *Enterprise* in 1815, making the trip from New Orleans to Louisville in twenty-five days. Within five years there were 60 steamboats, some designed to carry passengers, plying the muddy rivers that led to New Orleans. By 1835 there were 250 steamboats and some two thousand professional gamblers at work on them and in the dives ashore.

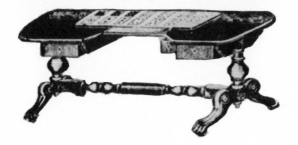

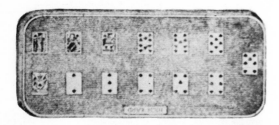

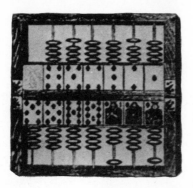

The professionals looked for suckers among the backwoodsmen, the rich planters, and the young sports. Inevitably, they became arrogant, convinced of their own cleverness and contemptuous of the suckers they fleeced. Such a situation was made to order for James Ashby, a lame gambler who didn't like pushy people. Ashby found a partner who acted the part of a naïve country boy on his way home after selling a drove of hogs. Ashby played the role of the youth's father, a fiddle-playing half-wit called Pappy.

With no encouragement, every gambler who met the pair set out to take them. The youth consented to sit in on a card game while Pappy played intermittently on his fiddle. It was several years before the professionals realized that Pappy was using the fiddle to signal his partner, who always got lucky when Ashby began to play. The team broke up, but Ashby reappeared later in St. Louis as the operator of the most popular faro game. No longer playing the hayseed, he now blossomed out in elegant clothes liberally decorated with gold chains and diamond studs. Reportedly, he carried a gold pencil set with diamonds that was the envy of gamblers everywhere. But his health was bad and he died while still a young man.

Another foe of the professional gambler was Jim Bowie, inventor of the Bowie knife and famous for his duels, his temper, and his strength. He enjoyed beating the crooked gamblers at their own game, and then beating them at his game as well. Perhaps his most famous exploit—until he died with Davy Crockett at the Alamo—was the time he boarded the steamboat *New Orleans* at Vicksburg and observed a team of sharpies at work on a young planter. Investigation revealed the planter was on his way home with his bride from New York where he had collected some fifty thousand dollars owed to his friends and relatives. The gamblers had heard about the money he was carrying and had started in on him at Louisville. Bowie, dressed in riverboat black, watched the process reach its inevitable end.

Faro equipment. In faro, players indicate on the layout which card they think will win or lose. The dealer draws two cards from the dealing box: the first loses, the second wins. Top to bottom: a table layout where representations of the thirteen cards of the spade suit are marked; folding board with layout; case-keeper; copper, and beside it a dealing box. Opposite page, trappers and flatboat men playing faro in the 1860s.

James Bowie, foe of the professional gambler. His famous ''Bowie'' knife was made from his own design by a blacksmith who had a method for tempering the steel to allow the blade to be as sharp as a razor. Commandoes and Rangers during World War II used knives based on this design. Below, Bowie and his knife during the Battle of the Alamo.

After stopping the victim from killing himself in remorse, he went to work. When Bowie flashed a huge roll in the bar, the triumphant gamblers stopped celebrating and quickly got a new game under way, with Bowie sitting in the sucker's seat. After winning and losing a few hands, the psychological moment arrived: Bowie was dealt a wonderful hand. One by one the others dropped out, after raising the pot, of course, until only Bowie and one gambler was left. By then the pot totaled seventy thousand dollars. As the gambler reached into his sleeve for the card he needed to win, Bowie seized his hand. At the same time he produced his famous knife.

The cheat was fully exposed. Bowie took the pot and no one raised the slightest objection, for Jim Bowie was even then a living legend. He returned fifty thousand to the young man, and kept the rest. That and a kiss from the bride was reward enough.

As boats increased in size and number on the rivers, so did the river cities multiply and become notorious centers of vice. The good citizens of such towns tried to ignore the brothels and bustout joints, maintaining they were necessary to cool the hot blood of sailors and thus protect respectable women from rape. Districts grew in each town where thieves, prostitutes, and crooked gamblers lived unmolested by the forces of law. Louisville had one such area and retained it until the 1937 flood, which scattered the prostitutes throughout the town, but Natchez, Memphis, and Cincinnati were equally infamous in the nineteenth century.

By 1830, settlements far from the river were disturbed by the arrogance and violence of these outlaws, and wild tales of outrageous happenings circulated. So when details of the Clan of the Mystic Confederacy became known in 1834, no one was greatly surprised.

VERY LATE FROM TEXAS.

"A sigh is heard on every gale,
A voice breathes from each *bloody grave*;
My country! hear they children's wail—
Rise and avenge thy MARTYRED BRAVE"

SAN ANTONIO HAS FALLEN!!
AND THE GALLANT BAND OF PATRI-
OTS,
who defended its walls with undaunted he-
roism, born down and overpowered, have
BEEN INHUMANLY BUTCHERED!!!
COL. DAVID CROCKETT
IS AMONG THE SLAIN—THE BLOOD OF
FREEDOM'S MARTYRS
CALLS ALOUD FOR REVENGE!!

By the documents below, the reader will find a melancholy confirmation of the rumors brought from Texas by Mr. William Butler of this place. To that gentleman we are indebted for a copy of the Declaration of Independence, and the documents which accompany it on our first page. The more recent intelligence below was brought express from Washington by Captain Benjamin W. Pedford of Sommerville, to whose polite attention, and that of Maj. Chalmers of this place, we are indebted for copies.

The announcement that appeared in contemporary newspapers relating the fierce engagement and fall of San Antonio. James Bowie and the famous frontiersman Davey Crockett were among the defenders, all of whom were killed.

Flatboatmen plying the western
rivers passed the long days
gambling and playing cards. A
detail from "Raftsmen Playing
Cards" by George Caleb Bingham,
1847.

It greatly resembled a modern Mafia "family."
The gang leader was John A. Murrell, a tall,
handsome killer with ambitions. He organized
the clan in 1832, and set Christmas Day
1835 as the date for revolution. His plan
was to cause a slave revolt throughout the
Mississippi and Ohio River valleys, under
cover of which his army of white desperadoes would ravage the principal cities.
The clan was governed by a Grand Council of
some one hundred senior outlaws. The army
consisted of fifteen hundred "strikers," and,
in addition, there were undercover agents
working among the Negro slaves. Funds
for the clan's campaign were obtained by the
crooked gamblers along the river, and were
used to buy arms and whiskey.

A Georgia man, Virgil Stewart, while posing
as a gambler named Adam Hues, was taken
to clan headquarters in a swamp across the
river from Randolph, Tennessee, and learned
Murrell's secrets. Returning to civilization, he
secured the outlaw's arrest on charges of
slave-stealing. Stewart testified at the trial
and Murrell was sentenced to ten years in

prison. Thereupon, the undercover hero
promptly wrote a best-selling book called
The Western Land Pirate. Like some modern
Mafia books, it is difficult to tell where facts
end and fiction begins, but the story created
a sensation. Stewart reported there was a
price on his head, and several attempts to kill
him were allegedly made.

Tennessee passed a law making it a crime to
play faro—believed to be the chief source of
the clan's funds—and a few gamblers were
tarred and feathered and ordered to leave
town. (This was called "lynch law," but it
was a milder version than the variety first
practiced in the Blue Ridge Mountains during
the Revolution, and certainly milder than
the "justice" later handed out after the
Civil War.) But with Murrell in prison, there
was no sense of impending danger. In June
1835, however, it was discovered that the
slave revolt was still planned and, in fact,
had been rescheduled for July 4, only a few
days away.

Word passed swiftly up and down the river,
and citizens formed committees of safety to

authorize companies of minutemen to start arresting every gambler in sight. One of the first men picked up admitted he was a grand councillor of the clan and revealed where arms were hidden. He was then hanged. Other arrests followed, leaders of the slaves were segregrated, and the planned revolt quashed.

Still the gamblers and their allies weren't intimidated. On July 4, riots broke out from Cincinnati to New Orleans. Stores were burned and heads broken, but the fore-warned citizenry put up a resolute front, and the clan had lost many of its leaders. Only in Vicksburg, the unofficial capital of the conspiracy, did things get out of hand. A band of outlaws set out to burn the town, but they were repulsed and retreated to their "district" on the riverfront. The citizens held a giant mass meeting that night in front of the courthouse and resolved that "all professional gamblers" be given twenty-four hours to get out of town.

The outlaws, contemptuous as ever of the majority, reasoned that this attack of civic virtue would soon pass and remained in their holes. The citizens gave them their allotted time and then moved in. In a scene not matched again until National Guardsmen cleaned up Phenix City, Alabama, in 1954, the "volunteers," as they called themselves, systematically raided every gambling joint and confiscated its equipment.

No resistance was met until the raiders reached North's Tavern, and there they were fired upon. When a respected physician was killed, the enraged citizens charged the building, dragged five gamblers into the street, and hanged them from the nearest tree. The gambling equipment was burned in the public square. By dawn every gambler had left town, many of them by canoe.

John Murrell (right), leader of the Clan of the Mystic Confederacy, an organization of gamblers and outlaws who planned to take over cities along the Mississippi and Ohio rivers.

Natchez followed suit in ordering out the professionals, and so salutary was the lesson of Vicksburg that hundreds left. Most of them went downstream to New Orleans where a more liberal attitude still held sway. Soon they were joined by refugees from as far north as Cincinnati and Newport, Kentucky, where mobs burned gambling houses. The swamp outside New Orleans became the hangout of many of the blacklegs and it remained a sanctuary for two decades. It was two years before gambling again became popular on the rivers, and when it did, the new generation of gamblers did their best to look and act like gentlemen.

The "uniform" of the professional gambler became a broadcloth coat reaching to the knees; dark, tightly fitting trousers; a low-cut, gaudy vest; a white, ruffled shirt; a colorful cravat, usually adorned with a diamond stickpin; and all topped by a broadbrim black or gray hat with a dashing curl in the brim. A large gold watch and chain were standard equipment, and rings set with diamonds or rubies were worn on at least three fingers of each hand. The diamond ring worn on the little finger by successful gambler-gangsters today is the part of the old tradition.

The gambler usually had a gun concealed somewhere in his coat, and perhaps a knife as well, for he made his living by cheating and had to be constantly prepared for violence. As George Devol, the most famous of riverboat gamblers, put it: "A man that will bet on such a game as monte is a bigger robber than the man who does the playing, for he thinks he is robbing you, and you know you are robbing him."

By "monte," Devol meant three-card monte, which was but a variation of the old shell game. The player usually worked with one or more partners. The victim was shown three cards—usually an ace, queen, and jack. The cards were then placed face down on the table and moved around rapidly. All the sucker had to do was pick the queen.

A night raid of members of a later and equally lawless clan, the KKK.

George Devol, most famous riverboat gambler and author of the classic *Forty Years a Gambler on the Mississippi.* Legend says the amounts of money wagered on the riverboats were fabulous. Devol claimed such accounts were "pure humbug." "I have grave doubts whether a brag of $2,000 has ever been won or lost at cards on the Mississippi."

Usually, one of the dealer's partners won a few times to show how easily it was done. Then, when another partner got the sucker's attention, the first partner either marked or crimped the edge of the queen. The sucker was quickly convinced he couldn't lose and was persuaded to bet heavily. He lost, of course, because the dealer simply palmed the marked card and replaced it. Sometimes the sucker could be persuaded to try again — on the grounds that he picked up the wrong card in his eagerness.

It was a simple game and intended, of course, to make the victim think he had a sure thing. In the hands of a Devol it was good for thousands on every cruise, for new suckers came aboard at every town along the river.

Devol may not have been typical of riverboat gamblers, but he wrote an autobiography that became the source of much of our information about that romantic breed. As a boy in Marietta, Ohio, he was rather a trial to his mother, enjoying such sport as shooting the cups off the table with his little bow and arrows as she prepared dinner for guests. At age ten, overgrown and a natural scrapper, he ran away. It was 1839, four years after the rebellion against gamblers and a good time to be taking to the river. He signed on as a cabin boy aboard the *Wacousta* at four dollars a month, and there his education began. By the time the Mexican War broke out, he knew how to "cheat the soldiers" and so cleaned up. Deciding it was time to go home "to the folks," he fulfilled every boy's dream. Loading up with four hundred dollars' worth of presents, including coffee, sugar, and tea, he took the *Hibernia* home.

"You ought to have seen me when I stepped on the wharfboat at Marietta, my birthplace, dressed to death with my gold watch and chain and a fine trunk I had bought in New Orleans for $40. I got my groceries off the wharfboat and hired a wagon."

Tom Sawyer would surely have understood Devol's feelings. But he stayed home only a year and had a fight nearly every week. Then it was back to the river.

Despite what Devol said, some games were undoubtedly played for high stakes. Sometimes games became so exciting they continued onshore after the trip was over. Right, a riverboat poker game. Below, an illustration from George Devol's book in which Devol himself makes a fast getaway during a gambling argument. Opposite page, a victim about to be fleeced. Passengers put up with gamblers as something romantic on a tiresome journey.

Riverboat passengers crowd
around a game. Typically, a victim
was allowed to win at first,
eventually being dealt a good hand
while the gambler dealt himself a
better one. The overconfident
sucker would be cleaned out.

It **was** not always a gay life. Sometimes Devol would find no money aboard and be forced to gamble for chickens. Once he won a number of live alligators. More than once he had to leave the boat prematurely, disguised as a preacher or an old man, in order to escape the wrath of men he had cheated. Often they fired at him as he waded through the mudbanks to shore. And sometimes he had to fight them tooth and claw.

Luckily, in such physical encounters Devol could use his head. He estimated his skull was an inch thick over his forehead, and he used that thickness to advantage by becoming the champion butter of the river. For most of his early life, he wrote, "sporting men of the South" tried to find a man to outbutt him, but never succeeded. His reputation became something of a problem, however, for, like the gunfighters of the West, every man he met was out to take him. But he volunteered for his toughest fight.

Devol was going upriver on the *John Walsh* when a fireman with a busted head appeared from belowdecks and asked for a whiskey. He told how another fireman had gone wild and started butting everyone in sight. Devol offered to calm him, and a match was quickly arranged. A string was tied across the room at butting height, and in the center, a ribbon from a bundle of cigars was arranged. The opponents stood five feet behind the string on either side, and on signal rushed forward to strike at the ribbon—and each other's head.

They came together with a crash, and the fireman fell like a stunned ox to the deck. When they lifted his head, blood gushed out of the nose, eyes, and ears. Devol, who didn't even have a headache, gave the fireman money to be treated at a hospital and the man was put ashore at the next stop. Then the champion collected his bets.

Beneath a gambler's tough hide allegedly beats a heart of gold. Devol offers ample evidence that this is true. There was the time when word passed that a poor woman with six children was aboard without money for passage. The gamblers passed the hat

Banco, a fraudulent variation of the English eight dice cloth, was popular on the riverboats. It was usually played with cards on a numbered layout, the numerical total of a hand dealt calling for a prize or bank. If a hand added up to twenty-seven, however, the player was required to wager a sum equal to that he might win. The sucker always lost.

and everyone contributed except one stingy old man. So after the woman had been given the best stateroom, Devol opened up his game of three-card monte and the first sucker who was taken, for eight hundred dollars, was "old stingy." He proved to be a bad loser and complained, but the captain had no sympathy.

"It always did me a great deal of good to down a stingy man," said Devol, "for I knew he would soon have more, even if he had to starve himself to get it."

But playing the gentleman wasn't always easy. Once on the *J. M. White* Devol noticed a man and wife and was able to lure them to the table. The man wasn't very interested at first, and it was the woman who saw, or thought she saw, the possibilities. She persuaded her husband to bet, and subsequently lose, five hundred dollars. Then, still convinced her husband was an idiot, she bet eighty dollars of her own. She lost, and suddenly the truth dawned. She pulled her husband away. Devol and his partner admired her spirit and decided to give back her eighty dollars. She was smart enough to understand their motive.

"I will greatly multiply thy sorrow by refusing to accept the money," she said firmly. But such setbacks were few and were compensated for on occasion when Devol could lure a preacher into betting and return his money with the advice: "Go and sin no more." In one instance, when he had won not only the preacher's gold but his spectacles and his stock of sermons, he gave only the specs and sermons back. No point in overdoing a good deed.

Came the Civil War, and profit was good until the conflict began to move down the Mississippi toward New Orleans. A group of gamblers formed Wilson's Rangers and equipped themselves with the best horses and most handsome uniforms their gambling profits could buy. Each day they mounted up and rode in formation out of the city to a distant drill field. Once there, and out of sight of the ladies who cheered their departure each morning, they dismounted and played cards. After a suitable time, they rode back to town to be greeted again by the beautiful women.

General Benjamin F. Butler, here and facing page, whose high-handed rule as military governor of New Orleans earned him the name "Beast." Among his other exploits, Butler confiscated all the horses at the racetrack, worth about $50,000. As the story goes, his brother and business partner then sold the animals to the Confederate Army.

Finally, however, war came closer. General Ben Butler was marching on the city and a federal fleet was anchored in the river. Wilson's Rangers mounted to the saddle and rode out to do their duty. At the first volley, however, they thought better of it. They turned their horses and raced back to town, but no one was making book. Once back in the city, they cut the buttons off their uniforms, buried their sabers, and tried to look like timid civilians. As Devol put it: "We had enough of military glory and were tired of war."

General Butler took over New Orleans on May 1, 1862, and, according to legend, stole everything including the silver spoons of the citizenry. But he permitted the gamblers to operate—all they had to do was cut Butler's brother in as partner. Devol got possession of the racetrack and was making money, but he robbed some of Butler's favorites and got tossed in jail. That was no disgrace, since some of the best people in New Orleans were in jail, and all had plenty of friends on the outside to keep them supplied with food and wine. Butler made an inspection one day and was enraged to discover that "those damned rascals are living better than I ever did."

Eventually, Devol was released and made his peace with Butler. "He gave me two silver spoons to remember him by," the gambler boasted.

With the end of the war, riverboat racing became popular, and captains vied with each other to set new records and outsail their rivals. Naturally, this produced a bit of betting on the side and led eventually to the race of the century—the celebrated contest between the *Natchez* and the *Robert E. Lee*.

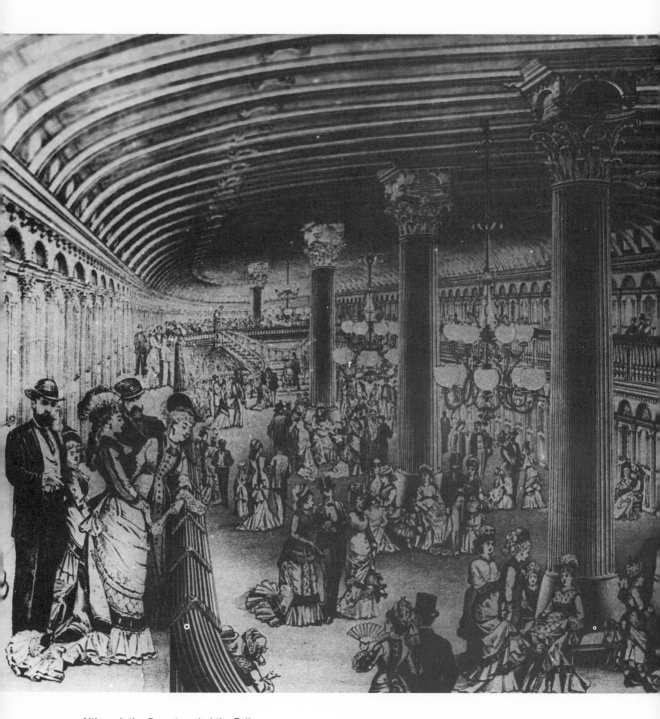

Although the *Drew* traveled the Fall
River line, the luxurious furnishings
of its great saloon were typical of
the Mississippi steamers.

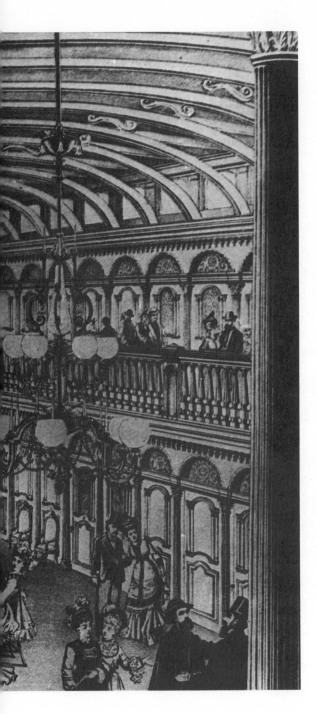

Captain Thomas E. Leathers, a reckless gambler who would throw slabs of bacon into the furnace in order to get a hotter fire, commanded the *Natchez,* which for some years had been queen of the river. But in 1866 the *Robert E. Lee* challenged that supremacy. Leathers promptly had a new *Natchez* built, and soon the press and public were demanding that the matter be settled in a race. The date of June 30, 1870, was selected and the buildup began. It wasn't confined to the Mississippi Valley or even to the United States; European newspapers printed hundreds of columns and dispatched reporters to cover the event. Sporting men in London and Berlin wagered on the outcome, and of course betting was heavy in New York and other American cities. In New Orleans, however, excitement reached a height never before imagined. The city was swamped with gamblers, most of them betting their emotions rather than their reasoned evaluation of the odds. Sentiment was about equally divided, and most bets were even money.

Captain John W. Cannon, master of the *Robert E. Lee,* was well aware that his competitor was tricky, so he decided to get the jump on him. Before the race he stripped his boat of every nonessential, including furniture and cargo. Only a few passengers who planned to get off at Cairo were accepted.

Leathers, seeing a chance to make some money, accepted both passengers and freight.

The race, from New Orleans to St. Louis, began at 5 P.M. The *Robert E. Lee,* stripped lean as a greyhound, got the jump on the heavily laden *Natchez.* By the time she reached Baton Rouge, she led by a full six minutes. Captain Leathers fed his firemen whiskey by the dipperful, but the regular stops he made prevented the *Natchez* from gaining. She was still six minutes behind as she reached the city she was named after.

A Currier and Ives print of the famous race between the *Robert E. Lee* and the *Natchez*. Actually, the boats never came this close during the race. Below left, Captain Thomas P. Leathers of the *Natchez* and right, Captain John W. Cannon who led the *Robert E. Lee* to victory. Both denied any intentions of staging a race and took advertisements in the local papers to this effect.

A CARD TO THE PUBLIC.

Being satisfied that the steamer NATCHEZ has a reputation of being fast, I take this method of informing the public that the reports of the Natchez leaving here next Thursday, the 30th inst:, intending racing, are not true.

All passengers and shippers can rest assured that the Natchez will not race with any boat that may leave here on the same day with her. All business entrusted to my care, either in freight or passengers, will have the best attention.

　　　　　　　　　　T. P. LEATHERS,

Je25—5t2dp　　　Master Steamer Natchez.

A CARD.

Reports having been circulated that steamer R. E. LEE, leaving for Louisville on the 30th June, is going out for a race, such reports are not true, and the traveling community are assured that every attention will be given to the safety and comfort of passengers.

The running and management of the Lee will in no manner be affected by the departure of other boats.

Je19—otf2dp   JOHN W. CANNON, Master

Top, the public cheering the *Robert E. Lee* on its way. Above, a race on the Mississippi between the *Eagle* and the *Diana*. The *Diana* was used as a troop transport during the Civil War before being dismantled in 1866.

After Vicksburg, the *Natchez* began to gain, but Captain Cannon revealed his big surprise: instead of stopping to refuel, he went alongside the *Pargaud,* a prearranged supply boat, in midstream. The two ships exchanged lines, pulled themselves together, and continued upstream while fuel was brought aboard the *Robert E. Lee.* The maneuver was somewhat similar to the manner in which modern bombers refuel in the air. When the job was done, the lines were cut and Cannon's ship raced on. At Memphis she was almost an hour ahead of the *Natchez,* and half the population was on the river bluffs to cheer her on. But fans of the *Natchez* had not abandoned hope, and new bets were made by the light of hundreds of bonfires.

The *Robert E. Lee* made its only stop at Cairo, and victory toasts were offered in anticipation. But, abruptly, disaster fell; the ship ran aground on a sandbar.

Cannon tried every trick known to rivermen to free his boat, and at last succeeded, but the cheers of his crew faded away as from around the bend came the shrill whistle of the *Natchez.* Now only a few hundred yards apart, the boats raced on.

Nature took a hand. Fog, thick and impenetrable, closed in. Captain Leathers, acutely aware of his duty to his passengers and cargo, blew off steam and tied up at the bank. But Cannon, applauded by his crew, steamed blindly, if slowly, on. Luck was with him, and after an hour the fog lifted. The captain was so tickled he turned a somersault: the race was won.

Six hours and thirty-three minutes after the *Robert E. Lee* reached St. Louis, the *Natchez* pulled into port. Although Cannon had won, Captain Leathers was accorded equal honor. He wasn't too downcast. If his scheduled stops and the delay caused by fog were deducted, he maintained, his running time was faster than the record made by the *Robert E. Lee.* Many agreed. In Europe, all bets were canceled, and in America the debate raged for years.

Fate Marable operating a calliope on the *J. S. Marable.* He assembled some great jazz figures in his Mississippi riverboat bands.

An attempt to recapture the glories of the past was made in 1962 on the Ohio River when two survivors of the age of steam, the *Delta Queen* and the *Belle of Louisville,* were matched. But, alas, despite all the ballyhoo, no one took the race seriously enough to bet on it. Their caution was justified since the larger *Queen* got so far ahead that reporters aboard—including this author—soon retreated to the cavernous dining room to help themselves to a memorable buffet. The *Belle* won the calliope contest, however, so the pride of Louisville was assuaged. And as the bourbon bottle passed, someone retold the story of Elijah Skaggs.

No aristocrat was Elijah, no gentleman planter with slaves to till his tobacco and harvest his corn. To tell the truth, he was just a redneck from out of the backwoods. But he had good eyes, a brain both sharp and patient, and he had ambitions. As a youth he learned to handle cards and managed to amass a few dollars, but instead of settling down like his brothers, he went out to seek his fortune. Nashville was his destination, and he arrived there wearing a stovepipe hat and a black suit and looking like an itinerant preacher. Folks laughed at him as they laugh at rednecks today, but he won their money. The river traffic had just become important; faro was the popular game. Skaggs was smart enough to

recognize the possibilities for cheating, and he made a long and careful study of all the tricks. By 1835, he was rich and getting richer, and the only thing that bothered him was the knowledge that there were more suckers than he could fleece. So he created a gambling syndicate: promising young men were taught the art of cheating and sent out in teams of two. Many of the students were relatives from back in Kentucky. Once the home folks understood the drill, they decided faro was as much fun as squirrel-hunting and much more profitable. Elijah paid expenses and took three-fourths of the winnings.

Still not content, Skaggs hired a tutor to accompany him on his wanderings, and he learned about literature, banking, and industry. And then he fulfilled a dream by buying a plantation and two hundred slaves to work it. The teams of gamblers were cut loose and told to make it on their own: Elijah Skaggs had become respectable, sir.

Alas, the dream! The Civil War came and Skaggs, an ardent supporter of the South, invested three million dollars in Confederate bonds. With defeat they became worthless, but more than money was lost. Elijah's heart was broken as the old order crumbled. It took him five years to drink himself to death.

They made good bourbon in those days.

Riverboat passengers watch the passing shoreline and river traffic, whiling away the hours.

2 "QUOTH THE RAVEN"

Insecurity he knew from birth. His father left his mother while he was still a baby, and she died within a few months. Foster parents raised him, but never adopted him. He had no friends as he grew up — for somehow he was different.

Upon entering the university, he began gambling. It seemed the only way to security and to the respect he craved. He lost, naturally, and kept playing in the usual desperate effort to recoup on a throw of the dice. As a result, he was forced out of school — a gentleman pays his debts of honor, doesn't he? And the University of Virginia was a school for gentlemen.

He became a drunkard as well as a gambler, sponging off relatives and finally marrying a thirteen-year-old cousin whose worship of him was soothing to his bruised ego. When she died after five years, he wrote a poem about her. Over the years he wrote other poems and some short stories — the critics laughed.

Still trying to capture the beauty of youth, he became engaged to a childhood sweetheart — now a widow. Virtually on the eve of his wedding, he died at age forty after a final fling at liquor and cards.

His name was Edgar Allan Poe. It was 1849.

One year before, gold was discovered in California, and, illustrating once again that gambling follows wealth instead of creating it, a lot of men as frustrated as Poe, but presumably in better health, headed west to San Francisco. Overnight, a city was created, dedicated primarily to entertaining — and robbing — the gold-hunters. As a writer of the period put it: "Gambling was *the* amusement, *the* grand occupation of many classes, apparently the life and soul of the place. . . . everyone elbowed his way to the gaming table and unblushingly threw down his golden or silver stake."

In search of souls to save, a minister came to San Francisco late in 1849 and inquired if he had any competition. "We had only one preacher," was the reply, "but preaching don't pay here so he quit and went to gambling."

So important did gambling become to the men of the West that some of them, at least, would have been rendered inarticulate if deprived of the slang associated with the games. Mark Twain, an observer of human frailties, has described in his book *Roughing It* what happened when Scotty Briggs went looking for a newly arrived clergyman.

"Are you the duck that runs the gospel mill

next door?'' asked Briggs.

The minister replied that he was "the spiritual adviser of the little company of believers whose sanctuary adjoins these premises."

Baffled, Scotty scratched his head. "I reckon I can't call that hand," he said. "Ante and pass the buck."

El Dorado, perhaps the most famous gambling joint of the old West, opened in San Francisco under a tent. A square building of unfinished boards replaced the tent. It was lighted with clusters of whale-oil lamps, and it rented for $40,000 a year. That was reasonable, since the daily "handle" often exceeded $200,000, and was seldom less than $100,000. Indeed, everything was expensive: lumber cost $500 a thousand feet, ordinary tacks sold for $192 a pound, whiskey was $30 a bottle, a boiled egg retailed for a least $5, and bricks were priced at $1 each.

Despite the cost, other gambling joints were constructed. By 1850 the town had a population of twenty-five thousand people and more than a thousand joints. Faro was the big money-maker, of course, since it offered unlimited opportunities for cheating.

Of the colorful characters that gambling bred, Bill Briggs was most talked about. He considered anything less than a silver dollar small change and unworthy of his establishment, so each morning he tossed all that had been collected the night before out the door. The boys of the town, some of them accomplished gamblers, always enjoyed this performance. But the man most envied was a nineteen-year-old who on three turns of the dice won $22,000 and walked away. He apparently left town immediately, for his name was not recorded. That night everyone was in a sentimental mood and at the Bella Union they sang that old sweet-sad song: "You'll Never Miss Your Sainted Mother 'Til She's Dead and Gone to Heaven."

Denver followed San Francisco as the second gambling capital of the West, and it wasn't long until a crusading newspaper appeared in town. *The Rocky Mountain News* insisted that the mile-high city was no longer a mining camp and its citizens should start acting responsibly. Certain gamblers objected and burned editor William M. Byers's house.

Edgar Allan Poe showed brilliant scholastic ability, but quarrels with his foster father over gambling debts put an end to his college career. Opposite page, the bar of a gambling saloon in San Francisco, 1855. Note the minstrel show in the rear.

Above, a Currier and Ives print of San Francisco in 1850. Right, one of the advertisements for a San Francisco-bound clipper ship during the gold rush period. Far right, prospectors at work during the 1849 gold rush.

MERCHANTS' EXPRESS LINE OF CLIPPER SHIPS FOR SAN FRANCISCO.
Passages 106 & 117 Days.

THE WELL-KNOWN   EXTREME CLIPPER SHIP

EAGLE WING

For Freight, Apply at once to   LINNELL, Commander, is now loading at Pier 16 E. R.

RANDOLPH M. COOLEY, 88 Wall St., Tontine Building.

Agents in San Francisco, Messrs. DE WITT, KITTLE & CO.

ROCKY MOUNTAIN NEWS

THE MINES AND MINERS OF KANSAS AND NEBRASKA.

CHERRY CREEK, K. T., SATURDAY, APRIL 23, 1859.

THE OPENING OF JAPAN.   ALPHABETICAL CONUNDRUM   THE WORLD WITHOUT   NICATION
                                                              BATH
NEWS.   The present age is   lized by the   Why is the letter A like a c
             rapid su   ts in th
             histor

Top, the banner of the first issue of
The Rocky Mountain News, which
took a strong editorial position
against gambling. Below, a group
of buffalo hunters with the paper's
crusading publisher, William N.
Byers, rear row, far right.

Interior of *The Rocky Mountain News* office in Denver showing some of the frenzied activity directed at getting out an issue. Note the weapons strategically placed around the room to fend off marauders.

He refused to take the hint, so they tried to burn the newspaper plant. Failing that, they captured Byers on the street, but with the help of a friend, he escaped. The gamblers rode back to the *News* and opened fire. The printers returned the compliment, and the gun battle grew louder. Some of the citizens Byers had been appealing to suddenly got the message, grabbed their guns, and came running. The gamblers decided their bluff had been called and galloped away. One was killed on the wing, hit by a shotgun blast. Another was captured. The citizens took a vote and by a narrow margin decided to run him out of town instead of hanging him.

Jefferson Randolph Smith, a Georgia boy, became Denver's first underworld boss. He was widely known as "Soapy" Smith, being a master of "the soap game," which was similar in principle to the modern punch-board. Soapy, in the presence of a crowd of suckers, would insert five-, ten-, and twenty-dollar bills beneath the wrappers of bars

of cheap soap. The unwashed paid as much as five dollars for the privilege of reaching in a barrel to select their own. They hoped, of course, to pick one with money affixed, but only the shills or "cappers," as they were known, ever did that. Still, the people got something for their money, and that made Smith a hero.

It was a con game basically, however, and Smith used similar talents to achieve power with the politicians. He used that power to shake down the big gambling operators, and with their money bought more influence. The officials following standard practice still adhered to in some cities demanded only that Denver *residents* not be cleaned out by Soapy's pals.

Two other Smiths started Soapy's downfall. His brother, Bascom, killed a gambler known as "Shotgun" Smith and appealed to Soapy for protection. The other gamblers didn't like that much, and refused to pay their protection money. At about that time a reform governor started cleaning up Denver's

political sewers, and Soapy decided it was time to slip out of town. He tried to organize a foreign legion for service in Mexico, but didn't get very far. The discovery of gold in Alaska sent him north, and for a brief period he bossed Skagway. Then the citizens revolted, held a protest meeting, and killed Soapy when he tried to break it up.

Men like Soapy, who grasp the reins of power by use of the bribe, usually get little publicity. The smart ones don't want it, well aware that it is the man in the public eye who attracts challengers and trouble.

Ben Thompson, for example, wasn't really a skilled gambler, but he was fast with his gun. This combination made him infamous—he was always being caught cheating and, upon being accused, shot his way out. A Texan, he wandered the West, killing at least a dozen men before being shot down in a theater in San Antonio. A coroner's jury found he had been killed by Joe Foster in a gun duel, but that didn't explain the five bullets in the *top* of his head. Unofficial observers speculated that Big Ben had been lured into an ambush and shot from a balcony.

James "Wild Bill" Hickok, although usually on the side of law and order, was another who became too famous. Arriving in Deadwood, South Dakota, in 1876 to do a little prospecting, he was murdered while playing poker. Investigation disclosed too late that the murderer had been hired by the town's gamblers, who feared Wild Bill would be appointed town marshal. The killer, Jack McCall, spun a tale about a brother Hickok had allegedly killed, and so was released. But later in Laramie, Wyoming, he got drunk and boasted too much. Arrested, he was sent back to South Dakota where he was tried, convicted, and hanged. Hickok was avenged, and the aces and eights he held when shot became famous as the "dead man's hand."

If legend be believed, however, Wild Bill's gun continued to speak long after his death. It was given by Hickok's sister to another famous lawman, Pat Garrett, and was used by Garrett in his famous battle with William H. Bonney.

Born on New York's East Side in 1859,

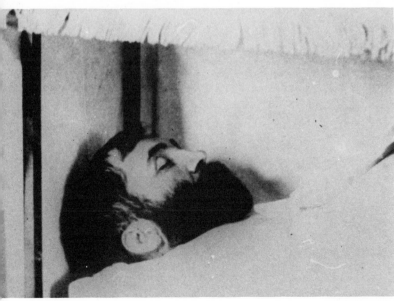

Opposite page, "Wild Bill" Hickok, marshal of roaring Abilene, Kansas, in 1871, gambled at the Alamo saloon. Hickok was so skilled as a gunfighter he would sit at poker games with his back to the door. When George Devol was dealer at Greer Brothers' Gold Room in Cheyenne, Wyoming, he attempted to cheat Wild Bill. Hickok made Devol give back his money, wrecked the room, and walked off with the contents of the cash drawer. Above, "Results of a Misdeal." Frederic Remington's illustration shows the type of gambling fights Hickok was often involved in. Left, Jefferson Randolph "Soapy" Smith in death. Soapy opened a gambling saloon called the Orleans Club in Creede, Colorado, in 1892, and organized a Gamblers Trust. As head of the trust, Smith took control of the town until finally booted out.

Bonney moved with his parents to Kansas around 1862. He grew into a skinny youth, about five feet, seven inches tall, with restless blue-gray eyes and a weak chin. A juvenile delinquent, Bonney was first arrested for stealing butter. Next he robbed a Chinese laborer of $70 and was put in jail. He escaped by climbing the chimney to the roof and jumping off. Guns and cards interested Bonney, and he practiced with one or the other at every opportunity. Offered a job running a monte bank in Mexico, he settled down there and was prospering. Inevitably, a local gambler challenged his honesty and started to draw his revolver. Bonney easily outdrew him, and put a bullet through his heart. From that day forward he was known as "Billy the Kid."

There was little time for gambling after that. Bonney killed twenty-one men—not counting Indians—by the time he was twenty-one, but then Sheriff Garrett killed him with a bullet from Wild Bill's old shooting iron.

Another famous murderer, "that dirty little coward," Robert Ford, met his reward in the Colorado mining town of Creede. Within two weeks of the discovery of silver there, a town numbering ten thousand people had arisen. Ford was one of the first on the scene. He opened his own gambling joint, Ford's Exchange, and began vying with Soapy Smith for control of the town. The rivalry ended when a mysterious stranger, one Ed O'Kelly, rode in and shot Ford without any preliminaries. While it was never proved, the popular theory was that O'Kelly had been hired to avenge Jesse James.

REWARD
($5,000.00)

Reward for the capture, dead or alive, of one Wm. Wright, better known as

"BILLY THE KID"

Age, 18. Height, 5 feet, 3 inches. Weight, 125 lbs. Light hair, blue eyes and even features. He is the leader of the worst band of desperadoes the Territory has ever had to deal with. The above reward will be paid for his capture or positive proof of his death.

JIM DALTON, Sheriff.

DEAD OR ALIVE!
BILLY THE KID

Left, Billy the Kid, prototype of the dead-end kid of the West, began hanging around saloons and gambling halls when he was in his early teens. Above, one of the reward posters for Billy the Kid that appeared throughout the Southwest, and at right, Pat H. Garrett who tracked down and killed the Kid after his escape from prison in 1891. Billy was twenty-two. A wealthy Easterner, Samuel Collins, bet a miner in Deadwood $5,000 that Wild Bill Hickok would be the cause of the Kid's death. Later, when both Wild Bill and the Kid were dead, Collins read that the gun used to kill the Kid had been Hickok's during his lifetime. Collins had won his bet.

$25,000 REWARD
JESSE JAMES
DEAD OR ALIVE

$15,000 REWARD FOR FRANK JAMES

$5000 Reward for any Known Member of the James Band

SIGNED:

ST. LOUIS MIDLAND RAILROAD

Top, reward poster for Jesse James. During his lifetime all train robberies west of the Mississippi were ascribed to him and his gang. Below, the popular version of Jesse's death. According to legend, Jesse was dusting a God Bless Our Home motto when he was cut down by Bob Ford.

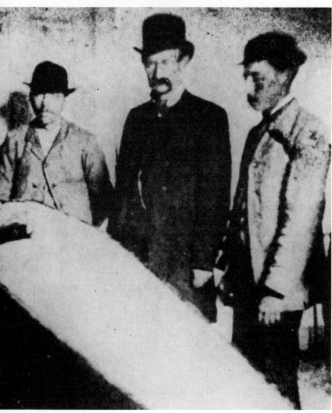

Outlaws Bob (top left) and Charley Ford were engaged by the local sheriff and the Missouri governor to kill Jesse James in return for a pardon for their former crimes and the $10,000 reward money. After fulfilling their side of the bargain they were granted the pardons, but received only $500 of the money. Left, the body of James was on public view in a St. Joseph undertaking parlor. "They have killed my sainted son. He is in Heaven," cried Jesse's mother. Above, Ed O'Kelley, the man who killed Bob Ford at Soapy Smith's hangout eleven years after Ford had gunned down Jesse James.

One of the dealers on that day when Ford cashed in his chips was a woman who achieved fame as "Poker Alice." Born Alice Ivers in England, she was educated at a fashionable southern school in America and went west with her parents. When her husband, a Colorado mining engineer, was killed in an accident, Alice became a professional gambler. Apparently she had picked up some tricks of the trade from her husband and his friends.

Her exaggerated British accent and the long black cigars she smoked both contributed to making Alice a frontier character. Her refusal to gamble or drink on Sundays added to the legend, and she could quote the Bible on occasion as well. Men considered her a smart poker player and there was continuing competition to beat her at her game. Occasionally she would visit New York for a round of shows and shopping, but inevitably, when her money ran low, she headed for the gold fields.

In her middle age Alice settled in Deadwood, and there she married and buried two more husbands. When the do-gooders tried to clean up that last wild town, Alice moved to Sturgis and concentrated on clipping soldiers stationed at a nearby army post. One night she killed a soldier, but pleaded it was all an accident. When the jury went out to deliberate, she sat in her cell and read the Bible. The verdict was the fashionable one of the old West—not guilty by reason of self-defense. When last heard from in the 1920s, the old lady was still operating a combination gambling joint and house of prostitution—and still quoting the Bible to Prohibition agents who came snooping around.

"Doc" Holliday was a gambler-killer who sometimes served as a police officer under Wyatt Earp. Not much is known about Holliday; he was a soft-spoken Georgian who acted on occasion as a dentist—thus the nickname—but he was a clever dealer of faro and a skilled gunslinger. It is no coincidence that a man who could handle cards smoothly

Doc Holliday, the "coldest-blooded killer in Tombstone," was a dentist who was more handy with a six-gun than his dental drill.

was usually adept at gunplay. Indeed, the two skills often supplemented each other. Earp, now a romantic figure in western legend, could shoot or deal with equal ease. With Earp, Holliday became famous in Dodge City, and he moved with him to Tombstone, Arizona, when that silver camp blossomed into the leading city of the territory. In Tombstone's glory days, gambling joints ran wide open on a twenty-four-hour basis, and there were no limits on the games. Holliday was a dealer in the Oriental Saloon and Gambling House. Earp was part owner, an arrangement much favored by gamblers who like to have the "law" on their side. Holliday carried two revolvers on his hips, a knife on his back under his coat, and, when deputized to assist the forces of law if not order, a sawed-off shotgun in his hands. The knowledge that he was slowly dying of tuberculosis — it killed him in 1887 — may have contributed to his ruthless and often reckless ways. He was widely feared and few cared to debate the matter when he cleaned them out at faro.

Earp, incidentally, lived until 1920, and died peacefully in San Francisco, a tarnished hero.

Another name that has lived in legend is Calamity Jane. An aspect of her life perhaps not so well known is that at fifteen, Jane worked for a venerable lady gambler men called Madame Mustache.

Wyatt Earp, top, in the 1870s and above, in the 1880s, when he was sheriff of Tombstone, Arizona. His greatest moment was the gunfight at OK Corral in which he, his brothers, and Doc Holliday put an end to a gang of murderers and cattle rustlers.

Nineteenth-century gambling
saloons. Opposite, one in Telluride,
Colorado, in the 1880s (note the
roulette wheel in foreground);
below, one in Sante Fe, New
Mexico, 1850s; above, a faro game
in the Orient saloon, Bisbee,
Arizona.

Two pictures of Calamity Jane who early in her career was a dealer in a gambling house run by the famous Madame Mustache. Calamity wore men's clothing and swore men's oaths. She claimed to have been the wife of Wild Bill Hickok, near whom she was eventually buried near Deadwood.

But Madame Mustache's fame owes nothing to the continuing popularity of that red-headed sharpshooter. Eleanore Dumont was her real name, or, at least, the name she was traveling under when first she appeared in Nevada City, California, in 1854. Young and pretty, she wore fashionable clothes and spoke five languages, but her past remained her secret. When she opened a gambling house a few days after her arrival, miners came from miles around to marvel at the woman's beauty and to admire the skill with which she dealt the cards in *vingt-et-un*—as she called the game known locally as blackjack.

Thanks to the presence of such a lady, men learned to remove their hats and to wait until they were on the street before brawling. Business boomed, and Miss Dumont hired a handsome young man to help handle it. All went well until the junior partner, David Tobin, offered a proposition: He wanted a bigger share of the profits or, barring that, exclusive rights to the lady's bed. Eleanore turned him down. On both counts. She believed with reason that she herself was responsible for business being good, so why give away the profits? Moreover, it was the fact that no one apparently had exclusive bed rights that made her so attractive to miners who, after all, lived largely on hope anyway. Tobin went east where reportedly he established a gambling house in New York and prospered. The young lady who spurned him became a wanderer, moving from camp to camp as new gold strikes were made and petered out. Always her attraction was her chastity, but as the years took their toll she lost her beauty and became Madame Mustache.

The "Madame" was not a tribute to advancing years but an acceptance of the fact that Dumont had indeed become a madam. When her own looks faded, she offered pert young things to pull in the miners. Installed upstairs above the gambling room, the girls could be counted upon to relieve the suckers of any gold dust that had survived the still nimble card fingers of Madame Mustache.

As the years passed, Madame's standards declined. Her establishments lost any pretense to elegance. Indeed, one account that survives paints an unattractive picture:

"The inside of the gambling house was worse looking even than the outside. The bar and the gaming tables were housed in one big downstairs room. A rickety set of stairs led up to a second-floor balcony where I saw doors leading to about a dozen smaller rooms. The place was foggy with smoke and smelled of sweating, unwashed bodies and cheap whisky. The floor was filthy."

The Madame herself was described: "She was fat, showing unmistakably the signs of age. Rouge and powder, apparently applied only half-heartedly, failed to hide the sagging lines of her face, the pouches under her eyes, the general marks of dissipation. Her one badge of respectability was a black silk dress."

In 1879, Madame Mustache took poison and killed herself outside of Bodie, California. The final blow, apparently, was the loss of her bankroll to a group of professional gamblers who teamed up to rob her. Left without money, love, or beauty, she decided the romance was over.

The money won and lost in the wide, wild West was peanuts compared to the profits of that insidious money-making machine known to its victims as the "Serpent" and as the Louisiana lottery to history. It was, said the New Orleans *Times-Picayune,* "conceived in the miscegenation of reconstruction and born in iniquity."

Typical Louisiana State Lottery tickets from 1889, 1891, and 1893.

Above, General Jubal A. Early and below, General G. T. Beauregard, Confederate heroes in the Civil War who were hired as administrators to give respectability to the Louisiana Lottery.

Actually a post–Civil War reconstruction legislature wrote a new constitution giving unto itself the "power to license the selling of lottery tickets and the keeping of gambling houses." Laws regulating gambling houses were soon repealed when the entrenched old-timers and their political allies objected to all the newcomers who flocked to town and sought licenses, but the lottery grew like a malignant cancer gone wild.

On August 11, 1869, the Louisiana Lottery Company was chartered for twenty-five years. Officially, the price was forty thousand dollars annually to the state for Charity Hospital in New Orleans, but un-officially it was understood that a great deal more would be paid in bribes. In later years, one legislator became famous as an "un-touchable"; everywhere that J. M. McCann went he found bundles of currency. Money dropped from windows at his feet, was under his hat when he picked it up, and under his breakfast plate. As much as twenty thousand dollars in each bundle. McCann returned it all to the lottery company and kept blasting away at them. But McCann was an exception.

In the beginning, the operators scored a master stroke of public relations by hiring those two deep-South heroes of the Confederacy, Generals Jubal A. Early and P. G. T. Beauregard. Each man was paid thirty thousand dollars a year and required to work only two days each month—an arrangement manifestly superior to Robert E. Lee's post at Washington College. Or so it seemed at the time. The use of respected senior citizens and elder statesmen to "front" for gambling projects has become standard operating procedure. (The hoods on Grand Bahama Island in the 1960s wanted Dwight Eisenhower to head their new casino there.) When Early and Beauregard died, the job went to ex-General W. L. Cabel, known to Texans as "Old Tige," but he only got six thousand dollars a year. By then the lottery was well established and didn't need reflected respectability.

The Louisiana Lottery octopus
stretching out its tentacles across
the nation.

By 1877, lottery tickets were being sold all over the country. There were daily drawings, except on Sunday, of course, for the benefit of New Orleans residents, and monthly drawings—except when the semiannual "grand extraordinary" drawings were held—for the benefit of the country. The lure, of course, was instant riches. In the semiannual drawings, anyone investing in a $40 ticket had a chance to win $600,000. No one ever won it, but a New Orleans barber collected $300,000 on a $20 ticket. (How much he was permitted to keep, if any, isn't a matter of record, but all gamblers know that a big winner now and then is good for business.) Most of the money came from tickets costing 25 and 50 cents, and the purchasers were those least able to afford it. The lottery offered hope, however, just as the numbers racket does today.

In order to keep faith with what might be called the more moral elements of society,

the operators of the lottery made much-publicized contributions to the public good. They gave $350,000 to turn a racetrack into a beautiful cemetery, built a library, and contributed heavily to the building of the Confederate Memorial. When floods threatened, the civic-minded gamblers were quick to donate money to build higher flood-walls and to wash the city's gutters now and then. Meanwhile, important public officials received contributions, and their relatives were put on the company's payroll. And still the money rolled in.

By 1889, the annual profit of the lottery was $13 million, and its mail provided half the work of the New Orleans Post Office. The lavish use of advertisements attracted many of the lottery's five million out-of-state customers. At the same time, the ads helped buy, if not the support of the nation's press, at least its silence. That is, until A. K. McClure, editor of the Philadelphia *Times,*

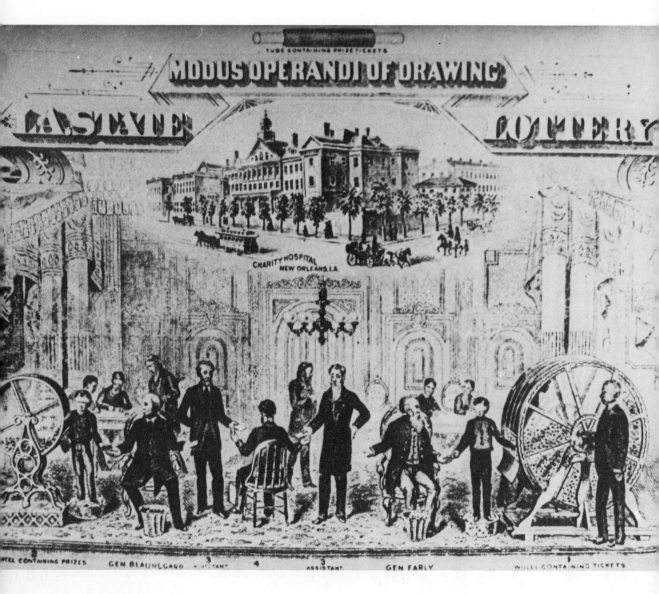

This illustration of the *modus operandi* of the Louisiana Lottery shows Generals Beauregard and Early and the young boys who drew the winning tickets, thereby giving the operation a note of honesty. Opposite page, announcements of various drawings which appeared in Louisiana newspapers.

pointed out that such advertisements were illegal under Pennsylvania law. The lottery company sued him for libel, then lured him to New Orleans where he was served with a writ issued by the federal district court in that city. He was trapped, it seemed, for the lottery company controlled the courts. But McClure counterattacked in the most effective way: he filed an appeal with the United States Supreme Court and demanded the right of "discovery depositions" as a preliminary to trial. The lottery company had no intention of answering questions exposing its secrets to the world, and it immediately backed down. What's more, it paid McClure $8,500 to cover his expenses.

This brazen attempt to intimidate the press boomeranged. Congress, after a hard battle, passed laws prohibiting lotteries from using the mails and banning newspapers carrying lottery advertisements from the mails as well. In Louisiana, reform-minded citizens finally concluded that they were being bought off with pennies while the operators took millions from poor people. A revolt began. The "Serpent" fought valiantly. The climax came on a bill to extend the life of the company's franchise which was to expire in 1895. After company officials offered $1,250,000 annually to the state, the bill passed, but Governor Francis T. Nicholls, a Civil War hero and no carpetbagger, vetoed it. To overcome the veto, the company needed the votes of twenty-four out of thirty-six senators. They thought they had them but one of their new converts went down to New Orleans for a good time and suffered a stroke. The doctors warned he shouldn't be moved, but his colleagues carried him back to Baton Rouge and announced he would vote from his sickbed. But the senator abruptly died. In a money belt around his body was found eighteen thousand dollars—the amount remaining from the price paid for his vote. The attempt to override the veto died with him.

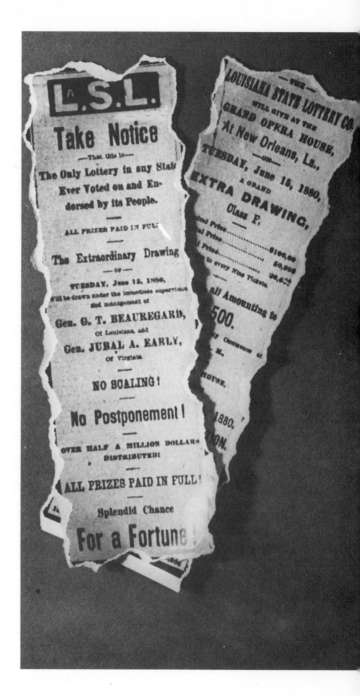

When the life of the lottery expired it was officially moved to Honduras where it survived for fifteen years. But the magic and influence were gone, and its agents were prosecuted when they tried to sell tickets in the United States. In 1907 the "Serpent" died. Its reputation had become so foul that the lottery movement in this country was dormant for fifty years. Of course its bastard son, the numbers racket, lived on, but it got little publicity. The gangsters had learned a lesion: Covert, illegal operations have certain advantages.

It was Mike McDonald of Chicago who coined the basic aphorism of the gambling industry: "There's a sucker born every minute." Chicago was a town of only six hundred people in 1835, but some of the refugees from Vicksburg and other Mississippi River towns found a haven there and with the Civil War, thousands of grafters and grifters wandered in. Michael Cassius McDonald was one of them.

Born in 1839, Mike was an accomplished gambler, thief, and politician by the age of twenty-two. So influential was he that his name was one of those used to persuade Irishmen to serve in the Union army. He contributed his name but not his service. Instead, he organized a gang of "bounty-jumpers"—men who enlisted under various names, received a bounty or bonus, deserted, and reenlisted under another name. Mike took a commission from each bounty collected.

As a gambling house operator, McDonald tried to look like the riverboat gamblers he admired, wearing only funereal black suits and white linen, but he lacked the polish. Nevertheless he had his codes: "Keep your word" and "Help your friends." He also had a pet hate: cops.

The hate stemmed from hard times beginning in 1869 when he personally cheated an assistant cashier of the Chicago Dock Company out of thirty grand. The cashier had to embezzle the money, and when caught, he fingered Mike's crooked game. Unable to raise sixty thousand dollars bond,

Opposite page, Mike McDonald (top), Chicago's political boss of the late 1800s and owner of the city's most popular gambling joint, The Store, and below, his associate Jim O'Leary, son of Mrs. O'Leary who owned the famous cow. After the great fire of 1871, shown above in a Currier and Ives print (the one the cow supposedly started), Mike McDonald's gambling operations took in $800,000 profit in one season. At left, a Chicago "rug joint" (luxurious gambling place) of the period.

Since they've existed, gambling joints have always been subject to raids from the law. Opposite page, a raid on an Indiana gambling house in the 1850s and below, police raid a New York gambling house in the 1860s. Above, publicity-seeking New York District Attorney William Jerome bursts into a rug joint around 1901.

Mike spent three months in jail. To win acquittal he had to bribe a score of witnesses, and the process took all his money. When he reopened his gambling house he lacked cash to pay the cops. Had they been patient he would have soon won enough, but they kept raiding him for more than a year. His violent dislike for the men in blue spawned a joke:

A solicitor: "We're raising a special fund, Mike, and we'd like to put you down for two dollars."
Mike: "Why do you need the money?"
Solicitor: "We're burying a policeman."
Mike: "Here's ten dollars; bury five of them."

The turning point in Mike's career came on October 8, 1871, when 3¼ square miles of Chicago was destroyed by fire. It apparently originated in a barn at the rear of 137 DeKoven Street where Pat O'Leary, his wife, and five children lived. One of those children was Jim O'Leary, a friend and associate of Mike McDonald and later boss of Hot Springs, Arkansas. One romantic tale puts the blame on the O'Leary cow, but the fire didn't start until well past milking time that night, so the tale is difficult to believe. More likely is another story, which has Jim and some of his friends shooting dice in the barn and causing the fire when they lighted a cigar and threw a burning match into the hay. In any event, the blaze that followed burned more than buildings—it destroyed the old political system. And in the new order that came along, Mike McDonald became the political boss. The Store, Mike's gambling center at Clark and Monroe streets, quickly became the most popular joint in town. The games were as honest as they had to be—that is, professionals and important politicians got a fair shake, but the naïve rich were taken as quickly as good manners permitted.

Gambling was centered on the second floor only of the four-story brick building. On the first floor was a saloon, and on the third and fourth floors a boardinghouse. In short, it was a supermarket of vice, but in those days such establishments were called "resorts." Something similar was popular as late as 1961 in Newport, Kentucky.

"Three of a Kind Beat a Statesman." Vice in Chicago during the 1870s. Opposite page, Mike McDonald would have been envious of one of Chicago's later bosses, Al Capone, who at his peak was making an estimated $25 million from his gambling operations alone.

Every form of gambling known to man, or at least to Chicago, was offered on the second floor of The Store, but roulette and faro got the most action. It was not, however, what was later to be called a "rug joint," that is, a place of luxury. It was designed for men who chewed tobacco.

Twice a year, The Store was raided by police—with Mike's knowledge and permission, of course. Accompanied by reporters, the police stormed in, busted up a few gaming tables, and arrested some "stand-in" dealers. The public conscience was satisfied, and business resumed within minutes of the police's departure. There was one real raid, however. Mike slipped up and permitted an honest cop, Simon O'Donnell, to become superintendent. O'Donnell sent his men in to tear up the place. Within hours, the superintendent had been reduced to captain—he was too popular to fire—and assigned to some post where he could do no harm. His successors got the message.

In 1887, a new mayor was elected on a law and order platform, and Mike decided it was time to go respectable. He closed down The Store, bought a newspaper, and invested in several legitimate and profitable enterprises, but his political power remained strong. And his married life provided enough excitement.

Mike's first wife, Mary Noonan, suddenly eloped with Billy Arlington, a minstrel singer. McDonald started after the erring couple and confronted them in front of the Palace Hotel in San Francisco as they climbed out of a carriage.

"Don't shoot, Mike," shouted Mary. "It's all my fault. Take me back, for God's sake."

Ignoring the frightened minstrel, Mike led his wife to the railroad station and bought tickets to Chicago. Once home, she resumed her place in society as if nothing had happened, and Mike was happy when she asked to have an altar built in their mansion. It was done, and a young priest, the assistant rector of the Church of Notre Dame, began dropping by regularly to assist Mary in her devotions.

Mike's pleasure ended abruptly one day in 1889 when he came home and discovered Mary and the priest had run away to Europe together. He smashed the altar and renounced Catholicism, then divorced his wife. Eventually the priest repented and entered a monastery. Mrs. McDonald came back to Chicago and opened a rooming house.

In 1895 Mike fell hard for twenty-one-year-old Dora Feldman, who as a child had played with his own children. He embraced the Jewish faith, married her, and built her a magnificent mansion on Drexel Avenue.

Twelve years later, Dora went downtown one day to the office of her lover, a commercial artist, and killed him with one shot from a revolver. It seems that the younger artist had begun to tire of the older woman, and she was afraid of losing him. Mike renounced the Jewish faith and, heartbroken, died soon afterward, but he did provide for Dora's legal defense, and the attorneys he hired got her acquitted. His friends whispered that perhaps Mike had been the biggest sucker of them all.

When McDonald retired from the rackets, his lieutenants proved unable to fill his shoes and settled instead for a piece of the action. The division of the Windy City into separate zones—West Side, North Side, South Side and the Loop—happened almost naturally, and not even Al Capone was able to put the pieces together a quarter of a century later.

"Big Jim" O'Leary was one such lieutenant who had come a long way since the O'Leary cow won undeserved fame. He fought a bloody battle for control of the gambling in Hot Springs, Arkansas, and helped establish that little resort town as a hideout and vacation spa for gangsters yet unborn. He had a spectacular failure on his record, too, when in 1901 he equipped a gambling joint at Long Beach, Indiana, some twenty miles from the heart of Chicago, and sent out engraved invitations which read: "You are invited to the finest equipped and only Monte Carlo in America, delightfully situated in Lake County, Ind., near the Standard Oil Company's Works at Whiting. No 'interference' from county or State officials. Open the year around."

A New York casino known as "The House of the Bronze Door" because architect Stanford White, who was hired to remodel it by owner Frank Farrell, installed a massive Italian Renaissance bronze door at the rear of the entrance hall. Opposite page, top, Chicago gambling fortress that operated for a short period during the 1900s. Below, the secret vault of a gambling house of the same era at 818 Broadway in New York.

HICAGO'S MONTE CARLO, A GAMBLING FORTRESS

A Costly Palace With Armed Guards, Fortifications, a Stockade and a Score of Carefully Trained and Ferocious Bloodhounds to Protect the Players from the Officers of the Law—The Long Struggle Which the Proprietors of the New Monte Carlo Have Had With the Moral and Religious Elements and With the Authorities of Two States * * * * * * * * *

VAULT CLOSED.   VAULT OPEN.

John Morrissey, former barroom brawler and pugilist, owned one of the most luxurious gambling houses in New York in the 1860s. He himself never gambled and only the enormous diamonds in the jewelry he wore suggested his profession. Opposite page, scenes such as this were not uncommon in the saloons Morrissey and his friends frequented before he made his fortune.

According to the blueprints, the place was a castle protected by stockades, barbed wire, armed lookouts, "man-eating" dogs, and alarm boxes, with tunnels leading to escape routes. The few visitors noticed that not all of the precautions actually existed, but the main trouble was the distance from town. O'Leary was ahead of his time; the development of gaming spots in the suburbs would not arrive until the advent of the Model T.

But if "Big Jim" was a visionary in some respects, his gambling joints on the South Side were extremely practical and they ran for many years. He had a part in a brief war with bookie king Mont Tennes and a few bombs exploded, but peace was soon arranged.

Tennes was a remarkable man and something of a pioneer in his field. Beginning on the North Side, he obtained a monopoly on racing information in Chicago by getting a franchise from the Payne News Company of Cincinnati, an early wire service. Using this as a handle, he forced every bookie joint in town to pay him a healthy percentage. In 1910 he organized the General News Service and forced Payne out of business. That extended Tennes's influence all over the United States, and when he retired in 1924 he left the field open to a man with even grander ambitions, one Moses Annenberg, about whom we will hear more later.

Needless to say, such men as McDonald, O'Leary, and Tennes could never have become rich or remarkable without utilizing political corruption. How well they were served is perhaps illustrated by a remark made by Police Chief George M. Shippy when O'Leary and Tennes were throwing bombs at each other. Said the chief:

"It looks as if there's a big gambler's war going on in Chicago, but I still maintain there's no gambling here worthy of the name."

In recent days it has been the practice for gamblers and their buddies to achieve a corrupt climate by using others. As Bugsy Siegel put it, "We don't run for office; we own the politicians." But in a simpler, less sophisticated day, it was possible to run for office—and get elected. John "Old Smoke" Morrissey is an example.

Morrissey was born in Ireland in 1834, but was brought to Troy, New York, when he was three. His father was a great scrapper, a great drinker, and a breeder of fighting gamecocks. By age eighteen, John had a police record for everything from burglary to assault with intent to kill and was the leader of a juvenile gang. He was also a good Catholic.

New York City was where the action was, and John was ambitious. In 1849 he sent a challenge to "Dutch Charley" Duane, a pugilist of note and a bully boy for Isaiah Rynders, a politician-gangster of some notoriety. He followed the message up by going to New York and to Rynders's hangout in person. Duane wasn't there, but plenty of other thugs welcomed a chance to beat on the upstart from out of town. Morrissey held his own in the free-for-all that developed, until someone slugged him with a brass spittoon. Rynders, impressed with the youth's courage and strength, nursed him back to health and gave him a job.

The nickname "Old Smoke" was acquired in a fight in a saloon with Tom McCann, a brawler of distinction, over the rights to the bed of one Kate Ridgely, a brothel-keeper. In the course of the battle, a lot of glowing coals spilled on the floor from an overturned stove, and McCann managed to pin Morrissey down on top of them. The smell of roasting Irishman filled the air. Someone threw a bucket of water on the coals. The steam blinded McCann and permitted Morrissey to get out from under. Once on his feet he busted up his opponent quickly, but his backside was still smoking, and the nickname was applied. With affection and respect, of course.

In 1851, Morrissey went west in search of gold. He made no effort to dig it, but settled down in San Francisco with a faro game. Although the profits poured in, Old Smoke became lonesome for New York. To finance the trip home in style, he entered the professional prize ring, defeating George Thompson. Instantly he claimed the title of

73

Left, James "Yankee" Sullivan and above, John Morrissey strike the classic poses before their championship match. Opposite page, the scandalous actress Adah Isaacs Menken whose scanty costume and skilled horsemanship were the talk of New York when she appeared in *Mazeppa* in the 1860s.

"heavyweight champion of America," and, back in New York, he proved his right to the title by defeating James "Yankee" Sullivan.

The bout was bareknuckle, each round lasting until a fighter was knocked or thrown down. Since each clinch ended in a wrestling match, fighters often won by throwing an opponent and falling heavily on top of him. At the beginning of a round both fighters were supposed to "come up to scratch" and "toe the mark"—in both instances a line in the center of the ring. If one was unable to come up, the other was declared the winner.

Sullivan prolonged the fight by "falling" whenever he got too tired, thus winning a respite between rounds. At the end of thirty-six rounds, both men were beaten and bruised but still on their feet. At the beginning of the next round, friends of Sullivan came into the ring to help their idol. Then Morrissey's pals climbed in and the prizefight degenerated into a free-for-all. The canny Morrissey retreated to his corner and watched the referee. Twice that gentleman called "time" and waited for Sullivan to join Morrissey at the mark. But Sullivan was having too much fun—or perhaps he had had enough of Morrissey. In any event, after waiting a full minute, the referee declared Morrissey the winner and heavyweight champion.

Morrissey fought once more, a childhood rival, John Heenan, who was known as the "Benecia boy." Heenan was married to that scandalous actress Adah Menken, who conquered more men with her *body* than ever did her husband with his *fists*. Morrissey beat this fortunate fellow in twenty-one minutes, and then retired to politics and gambling. The protection from police secured by one made the second possible.

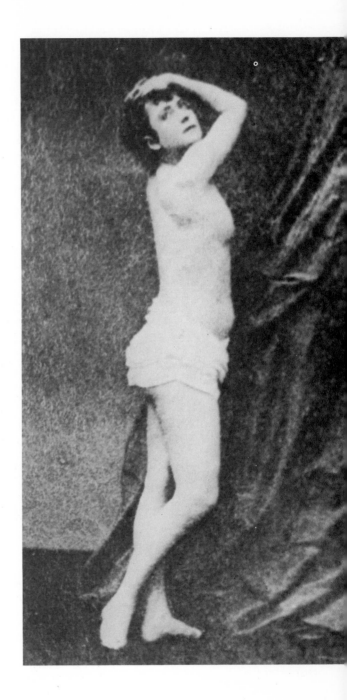

Top, the championship belt John C. Heenan, the "Benecia boy," brought from England. Below, the fight between Heenan and American champion John Morrissey took place at Long Point, Canada, on October 20, 1858. By accident, Heenan hit and broke his hand on a spike, and Morrissey was declared the winner. He refused to give Heenan a return match.

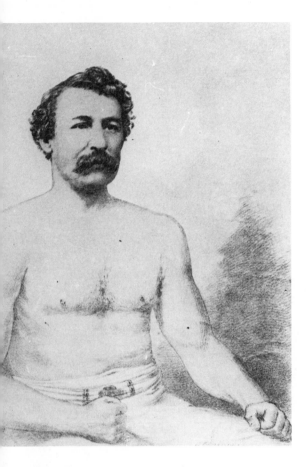

The "Benecia boy" was one of
Adah Menken's many husbands.

Attracted by Old Smoke's fame, the sports of
New York made his gambling house at 8
Barclay Street the most popular in town.
Morrissey counted a profit of $1 million in
five years at that location before moving
uptown to 818 Broadway. It, too, became
successful, but it was only a prelude to the
casino Morrissey built at Saratoga Springs,
New York.

That spa had long lured the wealthy. Prior to
the Civil War, Saratoga Springs was the
favorite watering spot of Southerners and
they gave the place much of its flavor. After
the war, a lot of *nouveau riche* tried to break
into society at Saratoga, and it became a
favorite vacation spot for the robber barons
of the "Gilded Age." Gamblers had always
been attracted to the spa, but Morrissey
recognized the true potential. Ultimately, the
Club House he built there was recognized as
the finest gambling establishment in America.
Replete with mirrors, flowered carpets, and
glittering chandeliers, the interior of the
building was nothing less than gaudy. Every
inch of darkwood, every piece of furniture
was carved, and lobbies and hallways were
choked with bronze figures. In the midst of
this magnificence hung a full-length portrait
of Morrissey: black mustache, gold watch-
chain, and black Prince Albert coat.

Women were permitted in the diningroom,
where caviar and *crepe suzettes* were
standard fare, and they also roamed the
various parlors and lounges. The casino
itself remained off limits, however, to both
the fair sex and citizens of Saratoga Springs.
Inside the casino, the rugs were thick,
cuspidors plentiful, and cigar smoke heavy
on the air. Dealers wore Prince Albert coats
and snowy linen, and managed the faro
tables, the roulette wheels, and poker games
with professional skills. A buffet to one side
offered quick refreshment, and a white-
coated waiter was always ready with a drink.

The ladies accepted the segregated status of
the casino, as ladies did everywhere in
America, but some male citizens of the town
grumbled at their exclusion. Morrissey
bought them off, however, with gifts to civic
associations and to churches. As one visitor
in 1871 put it: "He shared the profits of
sinning." The one thing gamblers have
always feared is a local revolt. As Sam
Tucker, a charter member of the Cleveland

Above, the main gaming room at Saratoga in the
1870s when it was run by Morrissey. Opposite page,
view of the Italian garden at Saratoga Springs
designed by architect Clarence Luce when Richard
Canfield became owner of the casino in 1894.

Above, Canfield's casino at
Saratoga. His house is at the left.
Opposite page, the former gaming
room of the casino.

Above, the gaming room at Saratoga. Under Canfield's ownership, Saratoga became the social rival of the resorts in Newport and Bar Harbor. At left, a photograph of Canfield during this period.

Syndicate, put it to the author in 1963: "We don't want to be where we're not wanted." By cutting in the locals with small gifts, Morrissey and others made sure they were wanted in Saratoga Springs.

Not content with the wealth and power he had, Old Smoke utilized his alliance with Tammany Hall to get himself elected to Congress. He served from 1866 to 1870, and contributed to the legislative process from time to time by offering to lick any representative who disagreed with him. Once he announced he could lick any ten men in the House, and no one arose to debate the matter.

Later he broke with Tammany and led a fight to oust William "Boss" Tweed. As part of his campaign, he ran for the state senate from Tweed's old district and won. When Tweed's successor complained that only a district that had previously elected Tweed would send "a vicious thug, a rowdy prize fighter, and a notorious gambler" to the senate, Morrissey ran for reelection from one of the most respectable districts in the city. And won. But shortly thereafter he died of pneumonia. After his death it was learned that most of his

wealth had been lost in the stock market as a result of his friendships with the robber barons who went to Saratoga in their private railroad cars every season.

One of Morrissey's early associates was more fortunate. Henry Price McGrath, a native of Versailles, Kentucky, was a noted hymn singer and church worker until he was suddenly bitten by the gambling bug. He moved to Lexington, center of the horse-breeding bluegrass country, got a stake, and sailed down to New Orleans in 1855. Profits were good until General Ben Butler took over the town. McGrath spent a year in prison and came out penniless. He teamed with John Chamberlain, a card shark from Massachusetts, and they went to New York where Morrissey let them buy into one of his joints. McGrath pulled out after two years, with profits estimated at half a million dollars, and he went back to Kentucky where he bought a horse farm near Lexington and settled down to become a country gentleman. In 1875, his "little red horse," Aristides, won the first Kentucky Derby.

McGrath had no difficulty in winning social acceptance. At McGrathiana, the mansion on

Aristides, winner of the first Kentucky Derby, was owned by gambler Henry Price McGrath and ridden by black jockey Oliver Lewis. The horse earned $18,325 during his career and ran twenty-one races, as many as Secretariat, whose career total is $1,316,808.

his estate, politicians and sportsmen mixed with gamblers and prostitutes. All were welcome. As a newspaper put it in 1872: "Not to know McGrath and McGrathiana is not to know all the splendors of the blue-grass country."

Meanwhile Chamberlain, backed by McGrath, built Monmouth Park racetrack as a competitor to Saratoga Springs. His clubhouse, a magnificent gambling joint, became internationally famous. However, he made the mistake of betting on his own horses and thus lost most of his wealth. But he helped prove beyond any doubt that the age of elegance had arrived.

Actually, the standards for casino quality were being set on the French Riviera in the little principality of Monaco. Overnight, Monte Carlo became the ultimate in fashion, patronized by kings and princes, by royal dowagers and royal mistresses. Americans who couldn't go to Monte Carlo sought the next-best thing closer to home.

Political developments were responsible for bringing gambling to Monaco. That this relic of feudalism owned by the Grimaldis survived into the twentieth century was due largely to the fact that the rocky stretch of coast was so barren none of the neighboring countries wanted it. In 1861 France annexed the only wealth-producing sections of Monaco, leaving Prince Charles III only 368 acres, most of it rock. How the prince would support himself and his large family when his French money was used up, he didn't know. His mother, Princess Caroline, suggested that he open a gambling casino. Since gambling was illegal in France and Italy at the time, if transportation could be arranged, a lot of wealthy suckers might come to play.

Four operators had accepted a franchise and failed before the prince brought in François Blanc. Of humble origin, Blanc had learned about gambling while working as a waiter in various European gambling clubs.

Top, Francois Blanc, who took over the concession to run Monaco's casino in the 1860s and literally transformed 368 acres of barren rock into one of the most valuable pieces of land in the world. He is responsible for molding the image of Monte Carlo that exists today. Above, Pope Leo XIII, who as Cardinal Pecci, was one of the first investors in the casino.

Above, the casino and Promenade des Anglais, Nice. The casino contained indoor gardens and a wide assortment of gaming rooms. Its season spanned the first four months of the year. Left, a school for croupiers. Pupils learned their trade during six months of daily instruction. Metal discs and pieces of paper took the place of actual currency.

The casino and below, the main gaming room at Monte Carlo in 1890. When Camille Blanc took over management of the casino after his father's death in 1877, he added a green dome and four Oriental minarets, making its architectural style truly eclectic.

Then he had learned to cheat in the stock market, had made a lot of money, and then spent seven months in prison for fraud and bribery. Upon getting out, he took his profits to Luxembourg and opened a casino. When it became a success, he was offered the opportunity to develop a grand casino at Baden-Baden in Germany. This spa attracted the wealthy from all over Europe, who came there to benefit from its supposedly curative waters. Unhappily, many of those who profited by the waters, or thought they did, lost all their money in the casino, and some killed themselves. It became something of a scandal in a world still dominated by the moral standards of Queen Victoria.

So it was that, in 1863, when Blanc was offered a new beginning at Monaco he accepted. Immediately, he was confronted with a crisis. A drive was under way to legalize gambling in northern Italy. Blanc launched an undercover campaign to convince the residents of the area that gambling was a dreadful vice. The resulting public clamor caused the government to ban the proposed casinos. Monte Carlo would have no competition.

Blanc then organized the *Société des Bains de Mer et Cercle des Étrangers* — the Sea Bathing Society and Circle of Foreigners. He sold stock, keeping enough for control. One of the first investors was Cardinal Pecci, who would later become Pope Leo XIII. But while residents of Monaco could bathe in the sea if they wished, they were not permitted in the casino. Once again, it was the visitors who were to be plucked. And while suicide was not made illegal — too difficult to enforce — the unwritten law was emphasized: A gentleman will wait until he gets home to kill himself.

Queen Victoria customarily visited the Riviera during the winter months. On one occasion the directors of Monte Carlo's casino found out that she would be driving through their country on her way to Italy and stood at the border holding armloads of flowers. Upon learning the identity of her well-wishers, Queen Victoria refused the flowers and ordered the doors and windows of her carriage to remain closed until she had passed through Monaco.

A grand new casino building and a magnificent hotel were erected on the rocky cliffs above the sea. A railroad was built connecting Monaco to the rest of France, and an advertising program made the place famous. Some neighboring resorts became jealous, however, and circulated stories about suicides, both real and imaginary. The grottoes below the casino were said to be stuffed with bodies. Boats were reported to leave the town twice a week with a load of dead gamblers to be dumped at sea.

Blanc fought back. Firearms and poisons were forbidden in Monaco, and employees of the casino were equipped with wads of cash to stuff in the pockets of any dead sucker they happened upon before they called the police. That way, the suicide could be blamed on romance and not gaming losses. But there were also reports that the people of Monaco were dissatisfied with their inability to share the casino's prosperity — apparently the visiting gamblers didn't bother to shop in town. Blanc settled those complaints by persuading the prince to abolish taxes for native citizens. That made everyone happy, and not even the earthquake of 1887 upset things for long.

The Prince of Wales discovered the delights of Monte Carlo, and, traveling as "Baron Renfrew," he continued to visit after becoming Edward VII. Allegedly, he fathered a lot of bastards under that pseudonym. Emperor Franz Josef of Austria-Hungary was also a frequent visitor and, despite his age, a playboy of renown. An Englishman named Carter Aubrey tried to set the emperor up for blackmail by arranging for him to meet a pretty Greek girl named Ilona. The emperor was willing, but his official mistress kept getting in the way. Finally the black-mailers kidnapped the mistress so Ilona could trap the emperor in a compromising situation. Aubrey broke in on them at the right moment, playing the part of the outraged husband, but it didn't bother the emperor, who left for Vienna the next day. Aubrey followed, trying to collect, and the emperor simply had him arrested and cast

into a dungeon for three months. Aubrey, feeling like the Prisoner of Zenda, agreed to apologize in writing, and was released.

Czar Nicholas II was another royal visitor to Monte Carlo who wanted to play, but his czarina kept persuading him that every sweet young thing he liked was really an anarchist bent on assassinating him. Or, if that didn't work, she would have police deport the girl. It was frustrating, but it was safe. And all royal Russians had safety on their mind in those pre-Revolutionary days. The Grand Duke Vladimir, twice wounded by would-be assassins, was given a police inspector as a private bodyguard on his trips to the Riviera. One night the duke heard a slight noise downstairs. He grabbed a heavy object, crept silently down the stairs, and hit a man he found crouching in the shadows. Upon turning on the lights, he found he had killed his police inspector, who had been unwrapping a sandwich. The Duke paid 200,000 francs to keep the story out of the newspapers.

Leopold II of Belgium was luckier than the czar—his queen had given up and didn't try to interfere with his love life. But Monaco police were always on the alert for the king, who had a habit of kidnapping women he wanted. Eventually, when sixty-five years old and a widower, he met his match in Caroline Delacroix, a waitress with ambitions. He agreed to a morganatic marriage—one in which the children, if any, get neither title nor property—but when the church criticized the marriage, Leopold responded by making his wife the Baroness Vaughan.

Roulette became the glamour game at Monte Carlo and remains a favorite of women today. Its origins are obscure. Some say it was invented in China. Others credit it to the French scientist Blaise Pascal, who allegedly devised the game while in a monastic retreat. The heart of the game is the numbered wheel and the little white ivory ball that rolls around the rim of the turning wheel and drops into one of the numbered holes. In Europe the holes are numbered from 0 to 36, but in America the operators have increased the odds in their favor by adding a double 0.

Leopold II, facing page, had a fetish for beautiful women, gambling, and sharp creases in everything from his clothes to his newspapers which had to be ironed before they were delivered to him on a silver tray. Above, Emperor Franz Josef of Austria obstensibly visited Monte Carlo to be with his wife, the empress Elizabeth. Actually, they went their separate ways. While the emperor was chasing other women, the empress carried on her own love affairs or practiced acrobatics from the swing she had had installed in the bedroom of her hotel apartments.

Any ball dropping in the 0 or the 00 signals the croupier to rake in all bets for the house. A variety of bets are possible—on the specific number, on a combination of numbers, on odd or even numbers, and on the color of the hole—red or black.

A lot of titled persons enjoyed roulette at Monte Carlo, but it was an obscure Englishman, Charles Wells, who became a legend in 1891 when he "broke the bank."

Actually, Wells only broke the 100,000 franc bank at one roulette wheel. Casino officials, recognizing the publicity potential, draped the wheel in black while they slowly brought over another 100,000 francs so play at that table could resume. (A franc was worth approximately 20 cents.)

Later, Wells broke the table's bank again, and once more the black cloth was brought out. By then he was something of a god since everyone assumed he had developed an infallible system. A song, "The Man Who Broke the Bank at Monte Carlo," became an international favorite. Of course the sequel is seldom mentioned. Wells came back to Monte Carlo and lost everything he had won and much more. He went to prison for fraud and died broke. But the song lives and so does Monte Carlo.

It was thanks to James Gordon Bennett, owner of the New York *Herald,* that Americans began coming to the Riviera to gamble and observe the high jinks of royalty. Bennett had a villa on the coast and, longing for the company of Americans, began giving much play in his newspaper's society columns to those who dropped in. Soon everyone who could, did. And they returned home to tell others and to patronize the local pleasure palaces provided by the Morrisseys, the Canfields, and the Bradleys.

James Gordon Bennett Sr. and Jr. When one of Bennett's favorite Monte Carlo restaurants decreed that meals would no longer be served on the terrace, Bennett became so incensed he bought the establishment and hired an Egyptian waiter named Ciro to run it. As a result of Bennett's frequent references to it in his newspaper, Ciro's restaurant soon became all the rage among Monte Carlo society.

THE MAN WHO BROKE THE BANK AT MONTE CARLO

Words and Music by Fred Gilbert

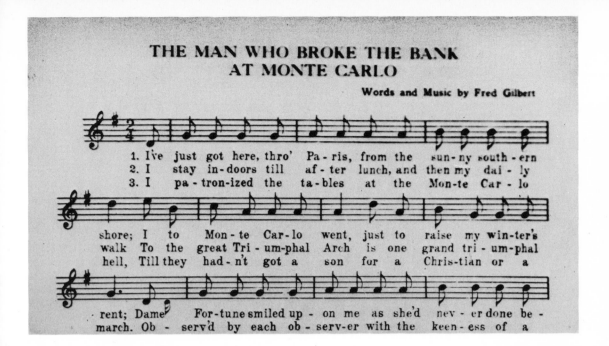

1. I've just got here, thro' Pa-ris, from the sun-ny south-ern shore; I to Mon-te Car-lo went, just to raise my win-ter's rent; Dame For-tune smiled up-on me as she'd nev-er done be-

2. I stay in-doors till af-ter lunch, and then my dai-ly walk To the great Tri-um-phal Arch is one grand tri-um-phal march. Ob-serv'd by each ob-serv-er with the keen-ess of a

3. I pa-tron-ized the ta-bles at the Mon-te Car-lo hell, Till they had-n't got a son for a Chris-tian or a

Top, "The Man who Broke the Bank at Monte Carlo" was a hit of the 1890s. Above, actress Lily Langtry, the most flamboyant of the mistresses of "Bertie," the Prince of Wales and later King Edward VII of England at right. Along with women and food, Bertie had a passion for baccarat which he played at the casino during his long social reign in Monte Carlo — a span of over thirty seasons.

Left, Mata Hari, the notorious spy, danced in the Monte Carlo Opera Company production of *Le Roi de Lahore*. Puccini sent her flowers and a card after her performance on February 17, 1906. Above, actress Sarah Bernhardt was a compulsive gambler and lost huge sums at the casino. One night she lost 100,000 francs and took an overdose of sleeping powder. A friend summoned medical help and saved her life. She never returned to the casino.

Above, famous
dancer Isadora
Duncan gave up
going to the casino
when she learned
that a young woman
had committed
suicide near one of
the tables. At left, the
Dolly Sisters, Rosie
and Jenny, were a
popular dance act of
the time. Jenny once
took great pleasure
in winning 15 million
francs from a
Hungarian nobleman
at the baccarat table,
for she stated that
her grandfather had
been a serf on the
nobleman's estate
and had often been
whipped by the
overseer.

Richard Canfield came into the world in
New Bedford, Massachusetts. His father was
a sailor turned publisher, but as he insisted
on being a Democrat when most of his
subscribers were Republicans, his son
Richard was forced to go to work at fourteen.
By the time he was eighteen, in 1873, he had
found his vocation in a poker room in
Providence. Three years later he had banked
twenty thousand dollars, so he went abroad
in the interests of his education. Monte
Carlo impressed him very much; he came
back broke, but with a vision.

In due course, Canfield found backers and
a partner, David Duff, and opened the
Madison Square Club at 22 West 26 Street in
New York. It was a good location, near
Delmonico's and several of the better hotels.
Most New York gambling houses, when they
weren't simply functional and drab, were
gaudy places. In the decorations of Canfield's
club, the emphasis was on dignity. Unhappily,
Duff was a roughneck at heart and began
causing trouble. Canfield locked his partner
out, then closed the house until Duff agreed
to sell his interest.

The house reopened on October 1, 1890, and
five years later Canfield had made a half
million and was looking for new worlds.
Ultimately, he bought Morrissey's old club
at Saratoga Springs which had fallen into
disrepute. He added an Italian garden and an
art gallery. Most famous portrait in the
gallery was that of Canfield himself as
painted by his friend James McNeill Whistler.
In the thirteen years Canfield operated the
Club House—from 1894 to 1907—the profit
was in excess of $2.5 million. And that was
achieved despite an annual operating season
of only six weeks.

Needless to add, the play at the tables was
for high stakes. Perhaps the most famous
episode still talked about concerned John
W. Gates, the barbed-wire magnate from
Chicago. Everyone called him "Bet-a-Million"
Gates, for he was a compulsive gambler
lucky enough to have a big bankroll. When
nothing else sufficed, he would bet on the
number of flies that might settle on a sugar
cube in the space of a minute, or which of
several raindrops coursing down a window
would reach the bottom first. On the day in

question in 1902, Gates was fighting a streak of bad luck. He allegedly dropped some $400,000 at the racetrack before adjourning in the evening to Canfield's clubhouse. Faro was his game, and in an hour and a half he lost another $150,000. Feeling certain that if he played long enough the law of averages would rescue him, Gates asked that the usual house limits on the size of bets be removed. Canfield was willing and Gates resumed play, doubling his bets. And his luck turned, as he had believed it would. Suddenly he started winning. He recovered the $150,000 he had lost at the table, and by closing time at 3 A.M. he had won $150,000. That made his losses that day a mere $250,000, so presumably he went home happy.

The game was the thing at Saratoga, so no one was overly concerned when Cornelius Jeremiah Vanderbilt suffered epileptic attacks while playing faro. As the second son of the super-rich "Commodore" Vanderbilt, he had certain privileges. He would lose consciousness for a few minutes while the game continued. Upon recovering, he resumed his betting—and his losing. His losses were estimated in the millions over the years. And his family contributed to Canfield's coffers as well. One day William Vanderbilt was waiting at the hotel for his date to come down. Across the plaza he noticed the casino and decided to invest ten minutes there. In that ten minutes, more or less, he lost $130,000. Easy come, easy go, he explained to the young lady when he joined her.

Still restless, Canfield decided to take over the Nautilus Club at Newport, Rhode Island. It permitted him another whack at the wealthy after the season ended at Saratoga.

Compulsive gambler John W. "Bet-a-Million" Gates, opposite page, who often played as long as forty-eight hours without stopping. To keep the peace when he lost, he would buy his wife expensive jewelry. When he won, however, his wife would make flapjacks, a favorite of her husband's from before his millionaire days. Top, William K. Vanderbilt, and above, Cornelius Vanderbilt II, grandsons of the Commodore, were among the members of the social set at Saratoga.

A rare photograph of Richard Canfield, right, with his manager, David Bucklin. Canfield acquired his extensive knowledge of art and literature while serving a six-month prison term for felony early in his gambling career.

Canfield was proud of his friendship with the well-known artist James McNeil Whistler, above, who painted the Canfield portrait shown here which Whistler facetiously dubbed "His Reverence."

Soon money was pouring in from all three gambling houses. He used part of it to furnish his properties with antiques and other objects of art. Typical was his pursuit of a set of dining room chairs.

In 1892 he had bought six Chippendale chairs in England and thought he had a complete set. A year or two later he stumbled on two more, obviously from his set. Suspicious now, he researched the subject and discovered the original group had consisted of twelve. A team of private detectives scoured England and Scotland. One by one the missing chairs were located and purchased. After Canfield's death, the full set was bought by a collector for sixty thousand dollars.

Meanwhile, Canfield established a new gambling house in a brownstone at 5 East 44 Street, New York, and spent a million dollars making it into the most magnificent private club in the world. It was known officially as the Saratoga Club, but unofficially it was "the house no one can close." Canfield had installed elaborate electric warning devices and stout doors to foil robbers and raiders alike. Moreover, no one was allowed in the gambling rooms until his identity and his credit rating were clearly established. For good measure, Canfield paid police quite heavily for immunity.

Nevertheless, as sometimes happens when gambling becomes a newspaper scandal, a reform drive began. A young man named William Jerome became district attorney on January 1, 1902, and he recognized that an antigambling campaign might make possible higher office. Much the same thing happened three decades later when Thomas E. Dewey followed the same route to fame. Jerome didn't make it all the way to Albany as Dewey did, but he came close. Using perjured information as a basis for a search warrant, he led a raiding party through a broken window of the Saratoga Club. He found no gambling and no indication there had ever been any. Actually, Canfield had been closed for weeks in anticipation of

The Newport restaurant Canfield House was the former Nautilus Club, a gambling house which Canfield opened in 1897. Never much of a success, he sold it in 1904. The profits for that season had amounted to a mere $1,100. Reggie Vanderbilt and some friends appeared the day after the house was closed and begged for one spin of the wheel. Vanderbilt put 1,000 on the red and won. Canfield ended up earning $100 for the season. Opposite page, top, the original gardener's cottage, stable, and laundry house in the 1940s and below, the building as it looks today.

Opposite page, top, one of the original gas lamp fixtures rewired and lighting the faded flowered wallpaper in one of the hallways below, the present dining room of Canfield House, with its vaulted, oak-paneled ceiling which once served as the main gambling room. At left, raised decorative tracery on the plaster ceiling and one of the fireplaces.

William Travers Jerome, the New York district attorney who persistently referred to the courtly and elegant Canfield as a "common felon."

a raid, but his high-class customers had kept the secret to themselves. It looked like a dry run for Jerome until his men found a secret room full of gambling equipment and thus had a case.

Some wheeling and dealing was necessary before Canfield paid a one-thousand-dollar fine and squared himself with the law. But the publicity helped fuel the reform drive, and laws were passed making wide-open casino gambling a risky affair. The reform sentiment spread to Saratoga, forcing Canfield to close the clubhouse in 1906. Shortly afterward he sold it and his other holdings.

He died in 1914 from the effects of a fall in the subway. Losses in the stock market had cut his fortune from an estimated $13 million when he stopped gambling to less than $900,000.

Some observers insisted that Canfield was unique—an honest gambler. The fact that he made so much money, they added, simply proves it isn't necessary to cheat, since the odds favor the house. Perhaps he was honest in his fashion, but he is remembered today as the man who invented the card game known as solitaire. And that tells a lot about the man.

Some writers like to moan that the age of elegance died with Canfield, and after that came the crime syndicate. But New York isn't the country, something gamblers and gangsters know very well, and the spirit of Canfield lived on in the South for quite a while in the person of Edward Riley Bradley.

Bradley was called "Colonel," but his title was the sort that anyone knowing a Kentucky politician could obtain. In later years he liked to boast about capturing Geronimo and playing cowboy in the wild West, but this son of an Irish steelworker began his real career as a bookie in Little Rock and Hot Springs, Arkansas. During the 1880s he was in Chicago, where he owned a hotel and prospered so at gambling that he was able to move to Kentucky and settle down like Price McGrath before him on a bluegrass horse farm near Lexington. His was the famous Idle Hour Farm, and four times in Bradley's life time its horses won the Kentucky Derby.

Canfield's original
New York casino was
at Twenty-sixth
Street, west of
Delmonico's. When
the restaurant moved
to the northeast
corner of Fifth and
Forty-fourth, seen
above with horses
and carriages parked
in front, Canfield
followed. (A star on
the sidewalk marks
the casino.) The
clientele was
composed mainly of
multimillionaires, and
losses were often in
the hundreds of
thousands of dollars,
even higher when
Bet-a-Million Gates
played. At left, a
cross section of the
casino. Canfield
spent over $1 million
to decorate it and it
housed one of the
finest art collections
and most notable
libraries in America.

A newspaper artist's rendering of
the night Canfield's was raided.
Unable to get past the electronically
controlled doors, the police
smashed a nearby window.

"Courteous" Jerome Meets "Fine Fellow" Canfield in Polite and Gentlemanly Raid.

"HOWDY!"

The newspapers had a field day with Jerome over his polite attitude towards the gambler and his house. Left, Jerome's answer to the New York *World* about the relationship between New York City law enforcement and gambling.

The newspaper clipping reads:

Corl...

"Circulation Books Open t..."

...AY, DECEMBER 12, 1914. ... P

NOTED GAMBLER KILLED
BY TUMBLE IN SUBWAY.

RICHARD CANFIELD, GAMBLER, IS KILLED BY FALL IN SUBWAY

Proprietor of Palatial Resorts
and Art Patron Trips on the
Stairs at 14th Street and
Fractures His Skull.

GREAT SECRECY MAINTAINED
ABOUT ACCIDENT AT HOME.

Was a Friend of Artist Whistler
and Owned $300,000 of His
Work at One Time.

Richard Canfield, biggest g...
and sporting man ever a c...
this country, a lover of art a...
friend of thousands of men ...
tional prominence, died yesterday
ternoon in his home, No. 506 Madi
Avenue, from a fracture of the s...
The fracture was caused by a...
Canfield suffered on the stairs
Fourteenth Street subway
Thursday afternoon. Ever...
parently was made to h...
subway accident and ...
illness of the noted gam...
until last night did the ...
come known.
Canfield was alone whe...
was picked up and ...
starter's booth in th...
he asked that "a f...
McKinley of N...
Street, ...

RICHARD M. CANFIELD
[From A Sketch]

BOYS' AERIAL ATTACK
...SES UP THE SKULE

Dropped

A newsclipping announcing the
death of Canfield, a man who never
himself gambled, once he had
established his casinos.

The Colonel became acquainted with Henry Flagler, who was developing Florida by pushing his railroad down the east coast toward the village of Miami. Occasionally, when a community along the route showed promise, Flagler would build a hotel. To please all of his customers he would then build a church and a gambling casino. When he built the Royal Poinciana in 1894—the largest wooden building in the world—at Palm Beach, he also built a chapel and the Beach Club. Colonel Bradley was asked to take charge of the latter.

Bradley made his own rules. The day of the free lunch was gone: The food would be of the very best, but the patrons would pay, and pay well. Only gentlemen in evening clothes who could hold their liquor would be admitted, and neither women nor local residents need apply.

Not surprisingly, the casino ended up in the red the first year. So Bradley took a giant step—he permitted women to gamble, and they proved to be reckless plungers. Hitherto, the casino had been a man's world, with women restricted to spacious salons nearby. Flagler disapproved, and had his trained preachers protest, but the Colonel refused to change his policy. In 1912 he built a new Beach Club, on the same simple lines as before but much larger. The octagonal gaming room was decorated in Bradley's racing colors—emerald green and white.

The casino was open only in the winter months when the best horses and the "beautiful people" came to Florida as regularly as the buzzards return to the Dade County courthouse in Miami. When spring came, Bradley closed the club and followed his stable back to Kentucky to prepare for the Derby. In the years the casino operated, no attempt was made to legalize gambling and, conversely, no effort to enforce the antigambling laws was made. Bradley owned Palm Beach's two newspapers, and his wealthy patrons controlled the local politicans and police.

Yet occasionally the Colonel was challenged. Best remembered is the time the pretty girl came to Bradley's office in tears one night. She pointed to a handsome young man just leaving the casino. That was her husband, she explained. In fact, they were on their honeymoon. Jack had insisted on gambling and had been cheated of several thousand dollars—all the money they had. Bradley took pride in the reputation of his club for honesty, and the accusations of the girl hurt. Without questions, he peeled off the sum she said her husband had lost and gave it to her. In return, he demanded that neither of them come back. The girl wiped away her tears and agreed. Next night, however, the Colonel was enraged to see the handsome Jack at the dice table. Upon rebuking him, he discovered he'd been taken—Jack was a wealthy playboy who had never heard of the girl and was unmarried. The Colonel apologized, and in later years enjoyed telling the story himself.

Palm Beach in those years between the wars became a symbol of wealth, of elegance, of exclusiveness, and the Beach Club was the heart of it all. That county sheriffs sometimes closed their eyes to other illegal activity on the grounds that the unwashed had the same rights to privacy as hoi polloi was a matter of no concern. Palm Beach was beyond political considerations— it had become a state of mind.

World War II brought changes. The Beach Club closed in 1941, and when Bradley died in 1946 the club's gambling equipment was dumped into the Atlantic at the Colonel's request. From then forward, people would look back on what had been and say with Poe's raven: "Nevermore."

No similar sense of nostalgia would be experienced by Chinese-Americans today, for in a little section of New York known as Chinatown gambling remains very much as it was a century ago. The players, however, receive more respect as individuals and as citizens than did their pioneer ancestors, who began coming to this country by the thousands when gold was discovered in the West. Transportation being what it was. it was cheaper to bring workers across the Pacific by boat than to send them across the continent by wagon train.

The Chinese, as Mark Twain found them in Nevada and California, were a rather servile group, eager to please, and excelling in the

Financier Henry M. Flagler visited Florida in 1883 and disgusted with the inadequate transportation and hotels, set out to improve them himself and so make the state a winter playground for the wealthy.

"Whitehall," the mansion Flagler
built in Palm Beach for his third
wife to the total cost of $3 million.
At right Flagler in the early 1900s.
Opposite page, the Royal Poinciana
Hotel, garden view, and below,
overall view, the largest wooden
structure in the world.

The Chinese gambling game Gee Fah utilizes a printing block which is inked to print variations on the numbers.

art of washing clothes. Their chief concern in life, he decided, was to make sure their bodies would be returned to China for burial. To that end, associations were formed whose sole function was to keep tabs on all live Chinese in America so that when dead they could be shipped home. Over the years, these organizations became known as "tongs," and they spread eastward across the country as the Chinese overflowed the mining towns and railroad construction camps. Gradually, the tongs began to regulate the new interests of the Chinese: opium and gambling.

New York's Chinatown dates back to about 1858, but it was ten years later when Wah Kee opened his vegetable store on Pell Street as a front for a combination gambling joint and opium den upstairs. Before long, the Chinese began pushing out the Germans and Irish who had first settled in that area near the Bowery. As the population increased, so did the gambling. Each tong regulated the action among its members, and, on occasion, conducted bloody wars with rival tongs. As far as the history of gambling in America goes, the Chinese action was never in the mainstream. Perhaps that was one reason it continued to be ignored. The New York *Times* noted in June 1975 that Chinese

gambling has been tolerated for fifty years "as a viceless form of recreation for the hard-working population."

Viceless or not, it involves money. Police in 1975 estimated the largest gambling dens in Chinatown had a weekly handle of $500,000. In April 1975, police confiscated $69,000 in just one raid. This isn't big money by casino or sports bookie standards, but it represents a sizable chunk of Chinese-American income.

Perhaps the most popular Chinese gambling game over the past century remains fan-tan. Some forty to fifty buttons are placed on a ten-foot-long table covered with black-and-white striped cloth. The players bet on how many buttons will be left when the dealer removes the majority four at a time. Thus, if forty-three buttons had been placed on the cloth, the winning number will be 3. The winner is paid off at odds of 3 to 1.

Some of the modern joints are located on Pell Street where Wah Kee opened his vegetable store. They are still protected by tongs, and well-armed gangs keep their eyes open for police raiders and local thugs. Other ethnic groups also have their unique ways of losing money, but none seem likely to rival the popularity of craps and poker.

3 SUPERMARKETS

It is a room without windows, twelve feet long and fourteen feet wide. The only furniture is a small cabinet and a chest-high rectangular table above which hangs a bright light.

The door opens. A man pushes a large metal cart containing three shelves into the room. The shelves are loaded with small metal boxes. Each box is about ten inches long, six inches wide, and four inches deep.

Two other men follow the first one into the room. They are middle-aged, fleshy, wearing dark glasses and dark business suits. The door is closed and carefully locked. One of the men takes a pad of printed forms from the cabinet and stations himself at the narrow end of the table where he faces the other men who stand side by side.

One of the metal boxes is taken from the cart and is unlocked by the first man. A mass of greenbacks and a few "foreign" chips spill out. The two men begin sorting the bills according to denomination. The range is from one dollar to a thousand, but there are more 20s than anything else.

When all the bills are neatly stacked, the man on the right begins counting the first pile. Abruptly he stops. His companions stare impassively as he claps his hands together sharply. Then he reaches into his pocket for a handkerchief, wipes it across his face, and replaces it. The counting resumes without a word being spoken.

When the first pile is counted, it is re-counted by the second man. If his tally

agrees with the first, the total is given to the third, who records it on his printed form, and the bundle of bills is shoved to one side. The first counter turns to the next denomination, and the process is repeated.

The third man drops his pencil. Without comment, he claps his hands together before bending to pick it up. Several times a bill floats to the floor—each time the man claps his hands before bending to pick it up.

When the contents of the first box is counted, the men proceed to the next one. The counting continues until the table is covered with stacks of greenbacks. When all boxes are empty, a currency separator is brought into the room, and the stacks of bills are loaded in it according to denomination. Then it is taken to the cashier. The counting room is locked until the end of another shift when once again the drop boxes will be removed from beneath the gaming tables and brought in for an accounting.

End of story? Not quite. For, mysteriously, thousands of dollars brought to the counting room in the locked drop boxes never make it to the cashier's office in the currency separator. Somehow, the money vanishes. The process is known as "skimming," and it can add up to as much as $4 million a year from a single casino.

One doesn't have to account for "skimmed" money. No taxes are paid on it, and there is no need to explain why large hunks of it go to men who are not owners of record of the casino. In short, skimmed funds represent the real profits of a legal casino—the cream off the top.

The counting room described here was in the Fremont Hotel and Casino in downtown Las Vegas in the days when Eddie Levinson was principal owner of record and ruling power. A graduate of illegal gambling joints in Detroit, Newport, Kentucky, and Miami Beach, Eddie achieved respectability in Glitter Gulch. So, naturally, when in 1962 his brother Louis was uprooted in Newport, Eddie wanted the same for him. He offered Louis a piece of the action at the Fremont, but Nevada authorities refused to license the Kentucky kinsman on the grounds he was "the notorious Sleepout Louie."

Eddie protested. The nickname, he said, stemmed from Louis's poker-playing habits. Games lasting from twenty to thirty hours weren't uncommon, and Louis hung in there until the end by the simple expedient of "sleeping out" a hand at intervals. He would simply rock back in his chair, close his eyes, and snore briefly, then wake refreshed to play on and on and on. Nothing sinister about that, was there?

If the truth be told, Eddie's background prior to Las Vegas was almost identical with his brother's, but even so, Nevada wouldn't buy Sleepout. Eddie remained respectable and Sleepout remained notorious. Five years later, however, a federal grand jury indicted Eddie on tax charges growing out of skimming activities at the Fremont. Louis, enjoying his enforced retirement in the plush resorts of the Caribbean, was too loyal to his brother to laugh.

Men such as Eddie Levinson have long boasted that if Las Vegas did not exist it would be necessary to invent it. There's perhaps more truth than is realized to that bromide, for before Las Vegas there was Agua Caliente, and only when it closed did Las Vegas begin its bizarre growth.

Paradise in the midst of hell was a good description of Agua Caliente, located south of Tijuana across the border in Mexico. An easy drive from San Diego, Tijuana advertised itself as "the wickedest city in the world."

Above, views of Tijuana, Mexico, which billed itself as the "wickedest city in the world." Top, the main street and below, part of the business district. Opposite page, Agua Caliente, south of Tijuana, gambling resort of the stars and other high rollers of the 1920s and 1930s. Top, the Country Club House; center, campanile and galerria of New Hotel, Hotel Agua Caliente; bottom, the Patio Hotel, all during the early 1930s.

Patterned after someone's conception of what a Spanish estate should look like, Agua Caliente provided green lawns, everblooming flowers, continental restaurants, a first-class hotel, swimming pools, stables, golf courses, and, most important, a glittering casino which offered every gambling game known to man.

Three American promoters and a Mexican governor built the resort on land owned by the Mexicans. It cost seven million dollars when it opened in 1928, and its proximity to Hollywood insured its continued growth over the next few years. It served as the one place the stars and starlets could let down their hair and play.

Especially popular was the Gold Room where millionaires played for the highest stakes. "High rollers," they were called because their favorite game was craps. To be invited to play in the Gold Room, and to be permitted to dine in the adjoining small restaurant where the service was gold, was proof enough that one had reached the top in his profession. It was a compliment to one's bankroll, and, of course, something to boast about. Such playboys as movie producers Joe Schenck and Carl Laemmle held private parties there.

But the casino in and of itself attracted top-flight talent—Clark Gable, Douglas Fairbanks, Charlie Chaplin, Jean Harlow, Mary Pickford, Tom Mix, Gary Cooper, Al Jolson, to name but a few. The games ran from 10 A.M to 5 A.M., nineteen continuous hours of action, and still some of the guests complained. Liquor was plentiful—champagne was cooled in garbage cans of ice—and, not that it was important, it was legal as well. Sports heroes such as Jack Dempsey and Babe Ruth dropped in regularly, and so did gangsters who were in the process of becoming folk heroes.

The coming of hard times in 1930 was not immediately evident in Agua Caliente. A golf tournament there in 1930 was billed as the biggest, money-wise, in the world. The Caliente racetrack opened the same year,

Famous patrons of Tijuana and Agua Caliente. Top, Babe Ruth playing golf, 1932; below, Jack Dempsey, 1931; opposite page, Clark Gable and Jean Harlow. Lower left, Tom Mix, lower right, Mabel Normand and Charles Chaplin.

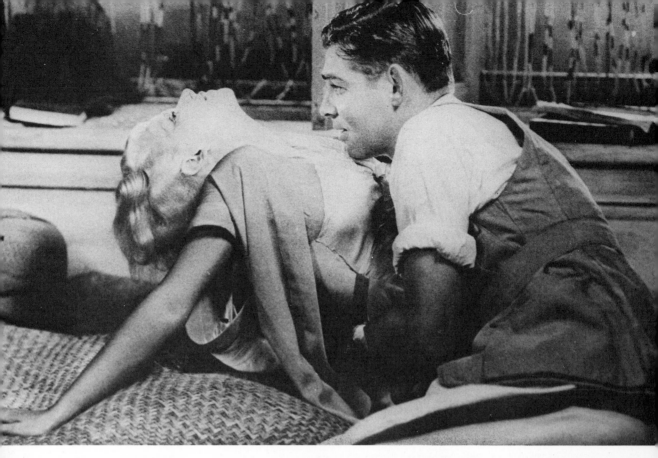

and offered prize money of $100,000 for feature races. On weekends the track drew more than eighty thousand spectators until, after a few years, rumors of fixed races and other funny business tarnished its reputation.

Perhaps a typical story to circulate in those glorious years at Agua Caliente concerned silent-screen-star Mabel Normand. Suddenly deciding to take a midnight swim in the nude, Mabel rushed from her room and across the lawn to one of the more distant pools. Unfortunately, she fell into a pile of horse manure which had been placed there earlier in the evening preparatory to fertilizing the greensward in the predawn hours when such essential maintenance would be least offensive.

One of Agua Caliente's respectful servants came to the rescue and found Mabel sitting in the stuff and gazing at it in amazed recognition.

"It is shit," she announced. "Common horse shit."

"Oh, no, Madam," replied the servant. "It is the very best grade available, I assure you."

"Thoroughbred shit," said Mabel sourly. "Well, it still stinks."

In 1935, Mexico suffered an attack of virtue, and President Cardeñas banned gambling. The friends of Agua Caliente tried to organize a revolution to overthrow such a puritan president, but without success. Eventually the unions seized the gambling casino in lieu of unpaid wages, and it was converted into a school and allowed to deteriorate. The race-track was reopened in 1937, and a succession of gamblers operated it for years. During World War II when competing tracks in the United States were closed, it enjoyed a brief return to prosperity, but the glow didn't last long.

Demand breeds supply. Since the stars of Hollywood could no longer journey south of the border for their fun, the Dunes near Palm Springs and the Clover Club in Los Angeles proper came into being to fill the vacuum. Both were plush and private, but they lacked that something extra so necessary to a movie mogul's ego.

Tony Cornero, owner of the *Rex*, largest ship in the gambling fleet off Long Beach. Opposite page, one of the notices posted aboard the *Rex*.

NOTICE!

More romantic were the gambling ships that appeared exclusively off Long Beach and anchored outside the three-mile limit. A long, wet boat ride was necessary to reach the floodlighted ships, and there was much talk of water pirates and hijackers. But once aboard, everything was pure pleasure: music, liquor, and rolling dice.

Tony Cornero was generally assumed to be the admiral of the fleet, but there were well-founded rumors that it was basically a syndicate operation. Once known as the king of the California bootleggers, Cornero was a true gambler—he would risk everything on a turn of the cards. The S.S. *Rex* was his flagship and it was staffed by well-armed goons who professed to believe that mysterious and uninvited boarders might attack at any instant.

It was the middle of 1939 before the sea battle developed. Dozens of deputies under the command of newly elected Attorney General Earl Warren swarmed aboard three of the ships and captured them without firing a shot. But the *Rex* was not so easily taken. The boarders encountered steel doors that prevented them from getting inside the ship. Before they could decide what to do, a concentrated volley from sea hoses drove them back to their boats. Warren, accepting the situation, ordered a blockade. Tony wasn't worried, since the ship was well provisioned, but he soon was confronted with a mutiny. A hundred or so guests abruptly decided the fun was over and clamored to go home. A compromise became necessary. If Warren would let the suckers get to shore, Cornero would permit an armed watch over his anchor chain—thus making sure he wouldn't put out to sea. Warren agreed, and the disgruntled customers were ferried ashore. Later, it would be something to boast about, but at the moment many of the men were hoping their wives had not seen the newspapers or listened to the news on radio.

Top, the *Rex*, the last word in
luxury. Water taxis discharged and
picked up passengers every ten
minutes. Above is the smaller
gambling ship *Tango*. Opposite
page, a rare photograph of the
gaming room of the *Rex*.
Everything from slot machines to
faro tables was used by the 2,500
people who boarded daily.

One of the shore taxis that Tony Cornero neglected to get licenses for and that caused the eventual demise of his gambling ships.

The confrontation off Long Beach continued for ten days as attorneys on both sides fought a legal battle. Cornero's people argued without rebuttal that the gambling took place outside California's area of jurisdiction—on the high seas—and fell into the same category as the "rum rows" that had operated off both the Atlantic and Pacific coasts during Prohibition. As a matter of fact, Cornero had done business in the Pacific rum row.

Warren didn't debate the point. His legal gimmick was the water taxis Tony had used to carry his customers out to the *Rex*. Somehow he had overlooked getting them licensed as public conveyances—it had never occurred to him that the state would stoop to such technicalities. Convinced, he agreed to pay a total of $13,200 in fines, taxes, and other expenses, and permit the destruction of all gambling equipment. Some 40 roulette wheels and crap tables were smashed, as well as 120 slot machines. Cornero sought solace in a high-stake crap game and managed to lose the *Rex* itself on a turn of the dice.

The sensation-seeking sophisticates of the make-believe world of Hollywood had to put up with makeshifts for almost a decade before Bugsy Siegel at last recognized their need and invented "the strip" outside Las Vegas. As a monument, it survives the man. Bugsy's well-publicized troubles may have begun when a pregnant cat was discovered in a pipe designed to carry water to a huge fountain that was to help make the Fabulous Flamingo a veritable oasis in the desert beyond Death Valley. Cats are notorious carriers of bad luck, and a pregnant cat— well, Siegel ordered it left alone. At the cost of delay and additional expense, the workman managed to complete the fountain by the day of the grand opening, but the cat had still not given birth, and Siegel made a hard decision: the Flamingo opened without its crowning glory, the fountain. Luck was bad. Due to the unfinished state of the hotel and an unexpected blizzard, fewer suckers than expected showed up. Of those who made it from Los Angeles, only George Raft lost heavily. The odds always favor the house, but in situations where the volume, or handle, of the betting is small, a casino can lose money for a short period if the

Special agents of the California
Attorney General Earl Warren's
office dumping the slot machines
from the *Rex* overboard after
Cornero surrendered the ship and
$24,900 to the authorities.

overhead is heavy. And the Flamingo, standing alone in the desert, had extremely heavy overhead. Soon Siegel was forced to close down. A few weeks later, when the weather improved and more hotel rooms were completed, he reopened. The cat had wandered away with her kittens, and the law of percentages went to work in Bugsy's behalf. The casino began making money. It made so much that the crime syndicate that had financed it decided to have Siegel eliminated. Rumor had it he was about to abscond to Europe with the casino's bankroll and his girl friend, Virginia Hill. More than a decade later, Meyer Lansky was skimming money off the top at the rate of four million dollars a year. The Flamingo was a gold mine, just as Bugsy had believed it would be.

Those inclined to take a gamble were not, of course, restricted to Hollywood. Across the nation there were plenty of people who enjoyed bucking the odds and flirting with the law, and they were willing to settle for surroundings considerably less pretentious than Agua Caliente. Gradually, the "sawdust joints" were replaced with "rug joints" on a regional basis as transportation facilities improved and driving became a national pastime.

One of the first such casinos was the Marine Room of the Riviera on a bluff just north of the New Jersey end of the George Washington Bridge to Manhattan. It served the entire metropolitan area of New York in the 1930s, and was as famous and almost as conspicuous as the Empire State Building. Fleets of limousines picked up customers at designated spots throughout the area and returned them hours later.

It was possible to dine well at the Riviera and enjoy the top-name entertainment without gambling. Indeed, no one was allowed into the casino per se without being frisked for weapons and identified for the record. Joe E. Lewis, who played all the nightclub casinos of the era, liked the Riviera best of all. But he was a close friend of Abner "Longie" Zwillman, the so-called Al Capone of New Jersey and the real boss of the Riviera. Zwillman was sponsoring Jean Harlow's career and allegedly selling her pubic hair to his friends. A single hair

Actress Jean Harlow, top, and below, her sponsor Longie Zwillman, gambling czar and racketeer.

enclosed in a gold locket was considered a trophy to boast about.

They still speak in whispers in New Jersey when they relate the tale of the mob figure Zwillman ordered taken for a ride. The guy knew a contract had been let for him, so he hastened to the Riviera and ordered the best dinner on the menu. His executioners arrived as he completed his meal, but, of course, made no move to take him in the dining room. When at last the waiter presented the check, the gangster left it on the table and walked over to the waiting hit men.

"Let's go, boys," he said. "The condemmed man ate a hearty meal."

And out into the night they went, leaving the unpaid bill behind. Across it the victim had written:

"Crapped out."

What the Riviera was for New York City and its suburbs, the Mounds Club was for Cleveland and its satellite cities. A Cleveland syndicate property, the plush casino in Lake County was operated by Thomas Jefferson McGinty. In 1930, McGinty was voted one of the five best-dressed men in Cleveland, but T.J. was a tough Irishman notwithstanding. A former boxer, he turned fight promoter when he realized the truth about the fight racket, and he branched out into horse racing. Once when his track in Bainbridge County was closed, the farmers of the area sent a delegation to protest. The price of hay, they pointed out, was falling fast and hay would soon rot on the fields if the horses didn't return to action soon.

The Mounds Club represented a big step upward for McGinty. It catered to the wealthy and provided top-name entertainment and good food, and although there were other casinos in the area, some operated by the same syndicate, none was in its class. It ran steadily for almost two decades, closing only during the winter months when, according to tradition, horses and high-rollers went to Florida. McGinty accompanied them, running various joints on Miami Beach such as the

Thomas Jefferson McGinty, owner of racetracks and gambling casinos from Cleveland to Miami and from Las Vegas to Havana.

Hickory House at 23 Street and Liberty Avenue. On the way north in the spring, he would habitually pause in wide-open Jeffersonville, Indiana, across the Ohio from Louisville, for Derby week. Then, sometime in the middle of May, he would reopen the Mounds Club for another long season of class entertainment.

It was September 23, 1947, a Tuesday, when the Mounds Club made history. The second show of the evening had begun shortly after midnight. The green-and-yellow dining room was crowded to watch Mary Healy and Peter Lind Hayes, the headlined stars.

In the middle of the act, a masked man dressed in a green GI fatigue uniform walked in from the kitchen. He carried an automatic pistol, and abruptly he fired it into the ceiling.

The audience assumed it was part of the act and began laughing in anticipation of high jinks to come. Miss Healy knew better — she ran into the rest room and remained there.

Three more men, hooded and grim, entered. Still the audience applauded. One has to assume the drinks served that night had been fairly potent. Another volley into the ceiling ended the laughter.

"This," said the leader of the hoods, "is no joke. Everybody sit down."

Carrying a submachine gun in his hands, one of the men went to the rear of the room, climbed up on a radiator, and stood there — the gun moving back and forth over the now nervous customers. The crowd sat silently as six more hoods came in and moved swiftly into the adjoining casino.

It was the practice in syndicate casinos of the era for the stars of the evening to lead the march into the gaming room after the show was completed in the dining room. Usually, the diners followed like sheep. On this night, the action had been more exciting than the show for about twenty patrons who had played while other dined. The intruders lined them up and removed diamond rings and wallets. Then the tables were stripped of their drop boxes and opened by Buck Schaffner, the club manager. On command, Schaffner opened the safe as well. It was loaded, containing not only the previous weekend's take but Monday's receipts as

Mary Healy and Peter Lind Hayes, performers at Cleveland's Mounds Club when it was robbed for the first time in its seventeen-year history.

well. Monday had been a legal holiday and there had been no chance to deposit the money in a bank.

Estimates of the total loot ranged from $250,000 to $500,000. The syndicate declined to give any figures. After all, gambling was illegal in Ohio. The newspapers were more candid, noting it was the first robbery at the club in its seventeen-year history.

Peter Lind Hayes proved he knew how to ad lib during the course of the robbery. Not having any money in his show business clothes, he borrowed forty dollars from the man next to him so the hoods wouldn't think he was "holding out on them." But the gang didn't overlook a bet—they looted the upstairs dressing rooms as well. When everything valuable was confiscated, the hoods calmly selected the fastest cars in the parking lot outside and drove away. The cars were later recovered and so were the six guards on duty outside—they had been locked in a shed.

Police, it shouldn't be necessary to add, were baffled—if they couldn't admit a casino existed, how could they acknowledge it had been robbed? Federal officials who, of course, had no "handle" in those days when the existence of syndicated crime was denied, said much later that the casino owners conducted their own probe and that the robbers were dead within six months. Modern reporters in Cleveland, who know less than nothing of the old syndicate and not much more about the new one, have been reluctant to accept this verdict. When occasionally they rehash the story of the robbery, they call it the perfect crime. Sounds more Robin Hoodish that way, and less businesslike.

In any event, it was more efficient than another caper in that area a few years before. In December of 1935, Harold H. Burton, later to be an associate justice of the Supreme Court, was elected mayor of Cleveland on a reform ticket. He brought in as safety director none other than Eliot Ness, who had attracted some attention as an alcohol and tobacco tax agent in Cleveland after being transferred from a similar job in Chicago. Ness wasn't a great investigator, but he did

Reporter Oscar
Fraley and the
man he made
into a legend,
Cleveland Safety
Director Eliot Ness.

have a certain flair for public relations,
despite a tendency to drink too much.

The crime war that followed got a satisfactory
amount of publicity, but it made little head-
way against the syndicate, which closed
its in-town joints and moved to the suburbs.
At least until County Prosecutor Frank T.
Cullitan got ambitious.

On January 10, 1936, Cullitan deputized
twenty-five private eyes, divided them into
two raiding parties, and swooped down on
the two most famous gambling casinos, the
Thomas Club and the Harvard Club. The
former, run by syndicate troubleshooter Sam
"Gameboy" Miller, gave no trouble. The
raiders seized gambling equipment, some
counterfeit money, and disturbed about five
hundred patrons. But the party hitting the
Harvard Club wasn't so lucky. James
"Shimmy" Patton, the manager, barred the
door and told the raiders," You can't get in
here without getting your heads bashed in."

No one wanted his head bashed, so the
deputized private detectives set up siege
lines and waited. After much delay, Cullitan
asked the sheriff for reinforcements, but
he was without ambitions and refused. Meanwhile, trucks and cars kept pulling up to the
back door of the club, loading up, and

departing. In this stalemate, the prosecutor
turned to Ness, who collected a group of
off-duty Cleveland cops and asked them to
volunteer to help the prosecutor. With
sirens screaming, Ness led them to the
rescue.

Reinforced now, Cullitan rapped on the
front door. This time he was admitted, only
to find that the club had been stripped of all
gambling equipment, money, and records.
The last van pulled out even as the office
was being searched, but no one tried to
stop it.

Although the next day Ness issued orders to
Cleveland police to arrest the casino
operators on sight, nothing came of it. The
syndicate continued to operate in the
suburbs and to expand into neighboring
states. Eventually, it expanded to Las Vegas
and Havana.

All of which didn't prevent Oscar Fraley, a
sportswriter of note, from making Ness into
a legend some years after Ness died. This
legend persists, and it is still repeated in print
today that it was Ness who ran the Cleveland
syndicate out of Ohio. Fraley's poetic license,
as he described it, has been relied upon by a
lot of writers with better motives, but of such
errors are history books replete.

The capers at the Harvard Club and later at the Mounds fade into insignificance, however, when compared to the action over the years at the Nacional in Havana. At one time in the 1950s—to keep a thread of consistency in the narrative—the men who owned the Mounds operated the Nacional.

A huge hotel, the Nacional boasted the largest casino in the western hemisphere—until El Casino opened in the Bahamas. Its modern history might be said to have begun in 1933 when it played a key role in a revolution.

Gerardo Machado had been dictator of Cuba since 1925, and both Cuba and the United States were tired of his excesses. Shortly after taking office, President Franklin D. Roosevelt sent Sumner Welles to Havana with orders to arrange a coup. (Things were simpler in those pre-CIA days.) Welles was told to act discreetly, of course. He did. A general strike was called, and on August 12, 1933, Machado decided discretion was the better part of survival and took off for the Bahamas. Order was restored and a made-in-the-USA government installed. It lasted just twenty-five days before being overthrown by Sergeant Fulgencio Batista y Zaldivar, who promptly promoted himself to colonel.

On October 2, 1933, a counterrevolt began which was centered at the Nacional. Batista's troops surrounded the hotel and poured in bullets and artillery shells. The walls of the building were pockmarked with holes. More than two hundred Cubans were killed before the rest bowed to military might. However, the casino continued to operate throughout the battle for the benefit of some bored Americans.

The dictatorship that followed was, in Batista's words, "mild, suave and sweet," and things got back to normal. So normal, in fact, that when Meyer Lansky, the syndicate-builder, appeared on the island he was able to do business. Batista decided he had much in common with the "Little Guy," and a friendship that was to endure for decades began. On behalf of the syndicate, Lansky invested in the racetrack at Havana and took over the casino at the Nacional.

Former dictator of Cuba, Gerardo Machado.

Above, the Hotel Nacional which housed an immense gambling casino. At right, Sergeant Batista and President San Martin congratulate one another after overthrowing Machado in 1933. In 1934 Batista ousted San Martin and set himself up as dictator. Opposite page, after the fighting ends, a Cuban revolutionary soldier counts the dead. Below, at the Presidential Palace Sergeant Batista reads a message to the people. Batista's overthrow of the Cuban government paved the way for Havana to become the Las Vegas of the Caribbean.

Even in those days of limited air travel, a lot of rich tourists came to Havana, and the Nacional paid off handsomely. Lansky continued to operate it until the war and German submarines prowling the Caribbean interfered. As he put it:

"We stopped when the war broke out because after that there wasn't any boats on the sea. And at that time you didn't have enough planes, and you couldn't live from the planes coming from Miami. You can't live from the Cuban people themselves."

When the war ended, Batista was in Florida where he had invested many millions. Lansky also understood the potential and built his new gambling empire in Dade and Broward counties. The flagship was the Colonial Inn, just south of Gulfstream Park. A rug joint equaling the Riviera and the Mounds Club, it attracted Hollywood stars as well as the kings of the underworld. On a given night, one might see Joe Adonis, Frank Costello, Vito Genovese, and Sophie Tucker, Groucho Marx, Joe E. Lewis, and Frank Sinatra. One might also see various state and national politicians. One could even see Sheriff Walter Clark, who operated an armored-car service which carried casino receipts to the bank in the early hours of the morning. The sheriff was a busy man; he also operated a slot-machine business out of the sheriff's office. Of course, he had his brother, the chief deputy, to assist him.

The success of the Colonial Inn and other syndicate establishments encouraged various independent promoters to take advantage of the official indifference to illegal gambling. As long as the efforts remained small, Lansky didn't object. Indeed, he subscribed to the belief that the more gambling and corruption, the better—up to a point, of course. That point was reached when Albert Bouche and John "Big Jack" Letendre opened the Club LaBoheme in a leased building near Gulfstream. It was a quality place, a competitor to the Colonial Inn, and, as such, could not be tolerated.

Patrons of the Colonial Inn, a casino near Gulfstream Park, Florida: opposite page, Sophie Tucker and Frank Sinatra; left, top and bottom, Mafia bosses Joe Adonis and Vito Genovese; above, Joe E. Lewis.

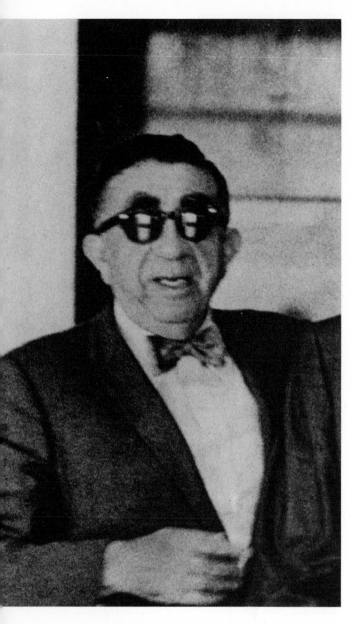

Jake Lansky, brother of crime syndicate boss Meyer Lansky, who ran one of his Florida clubs.

Bouche was accustomed to bowing to political and economic realities, but not Letendre. A politician from Rhode Island where he had been one of the founders of Narragansett Race Track, Letendre had an acquaintance with Butsy Morelli, a powerful Mafia figure there. Perhaps that relationship gave him delusions of power.

Shortly before the new club ended its first season, a stranger visited Emett Choate, attorney for Bouche and later a federal judge. Wasting no words, the visitor piled $250,000 in cash on Choate's desk and announced that the Club LaBoheme was under new management. Choate, forewarned that some kind of deal might be made, refused to accept the money.

"Better take it," said the stranger. "It's the best offer your people will get."

Letendre also received a warning. Disturbed, he drove down to Miami to consult with some of his friends. They treated him as if he were already dead. Alarmed now but still confident, he flew home to Providence to confer with Morelli. Much to his astonishment, the all-powerful Mafia boss refused to help.

"I shouldn't even talk to you," he said.

Letendre refused to admit defeat, and continued to seek allies. Shortly after midnight on April 23, he left the Blackstone Hotel in Woonsocket, Rhode Island, to drive to his "pretentious home," as the papers put it, in the suburbs. As his big station wagon slowed to turn into the driveway, a man stepped onto the runningboard, yanked open the door, and fired two shots from a .38 caliber revolver.

A neighbor heard the gunfire and looked out in time to see the killer get into "a dark sedan which immediately roared away" in the best gangster-movie tradition. Back in Broward County, Florida, Sheriff Clark laughed at the idea that local gamblers had anything to do with the murder. The real reason for the killing, he said, was Letendre's failure to pay a $45,000 gambling

The murder of John F. Letendre of Woonsocket, R.I., cofounder of the Naragansett Race Track and builder of the Club LaBoheme, would-be rival of Meyer Lansky's Colonial Inn.

debt up at Narragansett.

When the Club LaBoheme opened for business that winter, the man in charge was Lansky's humpbacked brother Jake. The club served very nicely thereafter in handling the overflow from the Colonial Inn. Everything went smoothly with "all saucy doubts and fears" now gone.

When Lansky's Florida casinos were shuttered in 1950 following the Kefauver Committee hearings, he helped Batista regain power in Cuba. The dictator was back in the saddle by 1952, but it was necessary to crush a revolt and otherwise consolidate his grip on the island before Lansky was ready to risk his capital. By 1954, however, the gambling boom had begun. New hotel-casinos to rival Las Vegas were erected. For himself, Lansky reserved the brand-new Riviera, and had himself listed on the hotel's records as manager of the kitchen.

The old Nacional was given to the Cleveland syndicate, Lansky's oldest allies. Sam Tucker

managed it, and as always, it was a money-maker. But Tucker was an old hand at sensing trouble before it developed. Long experience with illegal casinos had taught him to recognize the winds of change before they became a hurricane. Early in 1958 he concluded that Batista was riding for a fall. At a time when most U.S. officials and the press were writing off Fidel Castro as a phantom threat, Tucker began the process of extricating his group from Havana. The basic problem was how to pull out without tipping off the potential suckers. A non-Cuban excuse had to be found for selling.

The Nevada tax commission came to the rescue. It "discovered" that "the gambling element in Cuba has become an issue between the revolutionary parties and the Cuban government," and it ordered all Nevada owners of record to pull out of Havana. The order applied chiefly to Tucker and his associates, who operated the Desert Inn and the Stardust in Las Vegas.

Armed with this valid explanation, Tucker was able to unload the Nacional on Mike McLaney, a golf hustler out of New Orleans. McLaney was ambitious, but exactly three months after he became boss of the casino, Batista fled Havana with Lansky right behind him, and the old order crumbled. Castro let the casinos reopen for a time, however, and McLaney tried to cooperate. Unimpressed, Castro tossed him in jail briefly and again closed the casinos.

McLaney, always optimistic, returned to Miami Beach and awaited a new chance. He helped Lynden Pindling become premier of the Bahamas, but instead of the title of gambling czar he sought, McLaney was deported as undesirable. Unabashed, he made a deal with "Papa Doc," dictator of Haiti, to operate the long-shuttered casino there. Shortly thereafter, federal officials seized a shipment of crooked gambling equipment bound for Haiti, and then Papa Doc died. Mike, at last reports, was still hustling under the new leadership as thousands of Haitians starved to death in the treeless interior of the island.

McLaney isn't the only man to learn the hard way that bad luck dogs those in the "gambling fraternity" who try to operate on a big scale without syndicate permission. Huntington Hartford, the socialite and A&P heir, got the same message in the Bahamas when he tried to open a casino on Paradise Island in Nassau Bay. Despite spending millions, Hartford was completely blocked until he sold all but a small percentage of his holdings on Paradise to Resorts International, Inc. The men who ran Resorts had friends in the right places. Where Hartford had been stymied, they were able to get the necessary permits and a vast new gambling complex bloomed on the sandbar once known as Hog Island. Richard M. Nixon was a guest of honor when the casino opened in 1968.

Above, Fidel Castro whose dictatorship ended Lansky's successful business. Facing page, George Raft, Director of the Colony Club in London, takes over the operation of the roulette wheel in this 1966 photo.

Above, Bugsy Siegel,
who first saw the
possibilities of Las
Vegas, and his good
friend George Raft.
At left, Meyer Lansky,
who developed
gambling empires in
Cuba, Nevada,
Newport, Kentucky,
Florida, and London.

Owney Madden, the New York gunman "retired" to Hot Springs, Arkansas, where gambling equaled the waters in popularity.

The movement of syndicate capital to the offshore islands was part of a larger reaction to Robert Kennedy's battle against organized crime. As such long-running regional centers as Hot Springs, Virginia, and Newport, Kentucky, closed on the mainland, American gamblers crossed the Atlantic to England. New laws in 1960 legalized gambling in the British Isles and offered opportunities. Everything from dusty slot machines to the most talented "casino mechanics" were suddenly in great demand. And Scotland Yard, despite its fearsome reputation for efficient law enforcement, knew little about the whole business. What information it obtained came business. What information it obtained came at first from the FBI which, at the time, was obsessed with the Mafia! As late as 1965, Lansky's visits to London went undetected, but when some American carpenters were brought in that same year to do repair work at the United States embassy, they were held for hours by immigration officials who suspected they were members of the Mafia. Some of the carpenters, it seemed, had Italian names.

The development of casinos on a big scale in Britain was not planned. The bill legalizing gambling was aimed at enabling churches to raise money through raffles and bingo. But the legislation contained sufficient loopholes to permit private clubs to operate gambling, and it was easy to call a casino a club and sell membership cards at the door, much as had been done for years in the states where laws against gambling and liquor in public places were enforced.

The same techniques that had worked so well in Las Vegas were applied in London. One of them, the use of big-name entertainment stars as fronts, enabled aging actor George Raft to make a new beginning. Originally a flunky for Owney "the Killer" Madden—himself a British native—in Prohibition, Raft went to Hollywood in the thirties when Madden was courting Jean Harlow. He won a place in the gangster movies of the day, and continued to associate with "the boys" from back east. As his popularity as an actor waned, Raft was given employment by Lansky, at one of his casinos in Havana.

The Cubans were impressed with the old movie star. Reasoning that the British were just as naïve on the subject, Lansky arranged for Raft to front for the mob at the posh new Colony Club. Indeed, the name in lights was "George Raft's Colony Sporting Club." George was installed at the expensive Belton Towers. Each day a liveried chauffeur drove him in a limousine to the club at Berkley Square. It was all an act, of course, but the British loved it. To actually run the casino, Lansky employed a casino veteran, Dino Cellini. Dino was an old London hand, having previously organized and operated a school for dealers to supply the casinos of the Bahamas with reliable, and British-accented, personnel.

It was 1967 before British authorities, enlightened somewhat by a scandal in the Bahamas, wised up and began cracking down on known American gamblers. Lansky remained somewhat "mythical" to them, but they did expel Raft and Cellini as undesirable. By the time that happened, there were an estimated one thousand gambling casinos in Great Britain, half of them in London, and the influx of American dollars was adding stability to the badly strained economy. Gambling had become as necessary to England in the declining days of the British empire as it had earlier to the barren state of Nevada. The British were assured that the American gangster had been eliminated—the same story heard each year in Las Vegas. And, as usual, gambling fed on gambling. Legal bookie joints were next, and soccer became the sport to bet upon. As old values faded and the economic crisis deepened, the only people making money appeared to be the professional gamblers.

Meanwhile, back in the States, the drive to legalize more and more gambling continued unabated. Politicians, eager for new sources of revenue, accepted the notion that gambling taxes would be a painless way of obtaining money with which to maintain law and order.

The ancient and honorable term *sucker* is no longer employed. In polite usage, *pigeon* is preferred. In the supermarkets of organized gambling, pigeons are plucked.

4 THINGS MECHANICAL

I stood in the yard in a semicrouch and peeped into the window of the lighted room.

It seemed safe enough. The street, which ten minutes before had been full of people moving through the darkness, was empty now. A huge tractor-trailer parked in front of the house gave added protection. Far away a siren wailed softly. A warm breeze carried the sour scent of spilled garbage. The handbills I held advertised the Original Chicken Scratchers, some sort of a combo appearing at a local nightclub. The handbills would justify the presence of a strange white man in Miami's "Liberty City"—the black ghetto. I had passed them out earlier as I watched the crowds gather and the excitement build.

I was there to watch a bolita drawing, and that's exactly what I was doing as I stared through the window.

Inside the shabby room, a circle of men and women had formed. The only white face belonged to a man named Blount, the banker-representative of the operation known as the KY House. As I watched, he handed a small sack made of green cloth to the woman on his right. She shook it vigorously. It made a dry shuffling noise as if old bones were being shaken. Actually the bag contained small wooden balls, each a little smaller than a golf ball yet larger than a marble, numbered from 1 to 100.

The woman, her teeth gleaming in the yellow light, passed the bag on. Again it was shaken and again passed on. Around the ring it went, coming to rest at last with the woman on Blount's left.

This was part of the ritual, I knew. Technically, the shaking procedure was intended to reassure the audience that the drawing would be fair. But by letting each person hold the bag momentarily, the sense of excitement was increased. It touched drab lives with a bit of drama, and gave each participant a fleeting sense of importance.

Perhaps as many as ten thousand bolita tickets had been written for this drawing—at prices ranging from ten cents to a dollar. The persons in the room were there as observers, to attest to the honesty of the drawing, and as messengers to spread news of the winning number throughout the northwest section of Miami where the KY House was strong. Other bolita organizations around the city would be holding separate drawings for their patrons this midweek night—midweek so as not to interfere with the regular numbers action on Saturday. In 1965, when all this was going on, the citizens of the slums were offered two opportunities per week to bet their pocket change. Their total investment added up to an annual gross of millions.

Now Blount looked around the circle as

Legal lotteries have had a long history in Cuba. The examples seen here date from 1859 and 1878.

This figure emblazoned with lucky symbols and numbers appeared on a Cuban government placard telling the people to beware of forms of gambling introduced by the Chinese immigrants during the 1880s. Above, a Cuban street seller in 1946 displays the numbers he has available. One hundred tickets are printed for each prize. Should the customer buy the winning number, he would receive 1/100 of the prize.

Dreams for sale. Dream books for
the numbers games are currently
available at most newsstands in
New York City.

everyone grinned expectantly. Abruptly he
pointed at a white-haired man to his right.
The woman holding the bag cackled loudly
and tossed it to the designated "catcher."
The old man caught it in the approved
fashion, grabbing one of the balls inside the
sack and letting the weight of the others dip
toward the floor.

Smiling his approval, the white man stepped
forth to "tie off" the ball with a thick rubber
band. Blount was casually dressed, but his
slacks and sports shirt were somber-colored
and obviously expensive. The same compromise was evident in his grooming; he
wore his black hair cut short, but his
sideburns were fashionably long. Obviously,
some thought is given to appearance in the
strange world of the numbers racket. The
diamond ring sparkling on his pinkie was
another indication. One needed to look
prosperous but not formal, friendly but not
familiar.

After tying off the one ball, Blount poured
the other ninety and nine into another
sack. He tossed the original sack containing
the winning ball back into the center of the
ring. The noise of men talking and laughing
grew as Blount's helper, the "writer" whose
house was used for the drawing, took last-
minute bets. Action was furious for two
minutes, and suddenly a silence fell.

At that point I was interrupted and forced
to quit my vantage point. But I knew the
rest of it. Blount would slowly and solemnly
extract the tied-off ball and announce the
number written on it. He would leave it on
the floor for others to verify. And within five
minutes the number would be known
throughout that section. Next day the
winners, if any, would jubilantly present
tickets to their writer and collect on odds of
70 to 1. But there would be very few winners,
since the essence of numbers racket action,
be it bolita or some other variation, is to have
as winner that number which attracted the
fewest bets. In other words, Blount knew
what the winning number would be before
the drawing was held.

Various methods are employed to assure that the number drawn is among the "cold" numbers wanted. In Miami, the frozen ball trick is popular. A hollow ball filled with water is frozen before the drawing and inserted into the bag at the last minute. Instead of the bag being tossed to a "catcher," a member of the audience is blindfolded and told to reach inside the bag and select a ball. Needless to add, the person selected is part of the team. He simply feels around until he grasps the cold ball. Blount, however, needed no risky teamwork. A sleight-of-hand artist, he simply substituted balls when the time came to expose the tied-off number.

Some operators, less demanding or less skilled, compromise by simply making sure the "hot" numbers—those getting the most play—are not in the bag. Which one of the remaining numbers wins isn't all that important, so no additional hanky-panky is needed. Since certain numbers are always hot—always popular—the task of eliminating is made simpler. Once in a while, however, a hot number is permitted to win—just to stimulate interest and revive the faith.

The players make much use of dream books and other mystical hocus-pocus to select their numbers. This has not only made dream-book publishing a flourishing business, but it has given rise to a new profession—counselors who, for a fee, will go into a trance and predict a winning number. Typical was "Gooch the Root Man," who lived in the Coconut Grove section of Miami. He acted as a writer for a number of bolita houses, enabling him to sell a number after he had consulted "the spirits" and learned which numbers had the best chance of winning. Moreover, he

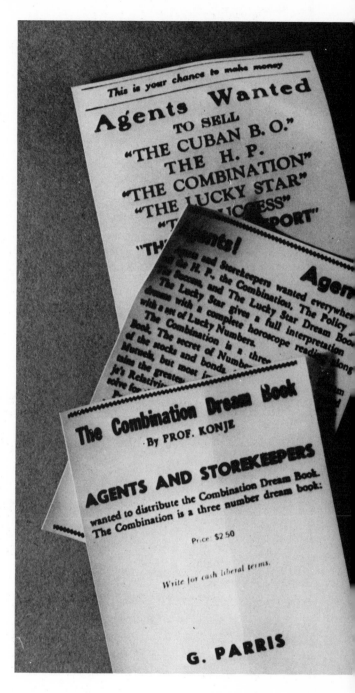

Ads for agents to handle dream books and related gambling sheets for bolita and numbers.

THE STATE LOTTERY.

The Name of a LOTTRY the Nation bewitches,
And City and Country runs Mad after Riches:
My Lord, who already has Thousands a Year,
Thinks to double his Income by ventring it here:
The Country Squire dips his Houses and Grounds,
For Tickets to gain him the Ten Thousand Pounds:
The rosie-jowl'd Doctor his Rectorie leaves,
In quest of a Prize, to procure him Lawn-Sleeves:
The Tradesman, whom Duns for their Mony importune,
Here, hazards his All, for th'Advance of his Fortune:

The Footman resolves, if he meets no Disaster,
To mount his gilt Chariot, and vie with his Master:
The Cook-Wench determines, by one lucky Hit,
To free her fair Hands from the Pot-hooks and Spit:
The Chamber-maid struts in her Ladies Cast Gown,
And hopes to be dub'd the Top Toast of the Town:
But Fortune alas! will have small Share of Thanks,
When all their high Wishes are bury'd in Blanks:
For tho' they for Benefits eagerly watch'd,
They reckon'd their Chickens before they were hatch'd

Engraven By B. Roberts & Sold by him at his Shop in Ball Ally Lombard Street.   Price 6.

144

Opposite page, an engraving showing a state lottery in England in 1739; above, a French lottery in 1907; and left, a ticket for a lottery in Washington Territory, 1876.

arranged to get all the winning numbers within minutes of the various drawings, and he posted them on his wall. After witnessing the preliminaries to the KY House drawing, I went to the home of Gooch to discover that the winning number that night at the KY House was a cold 68. At the suggestion of my guide, I left a dollar for Gooch, who was either in a trance or sleeping off a drunk—I couldn't tell which.

For many years, a rival of bolita along the Florida Gold Coast was the numbers game based on the Cuban National Lottery. Each Saturday in Havana an elaborate ceremony took place. Winning numbers were drawn from a drum holding 46,000 numbered balls, and from a smaller drum were drawn in random order balls listing the amount of the prizes. There were literally hundreds of prizes, and no one knew when the first of five top prizes worth ten thousand dollars each would pop out.

The entire affair was broadcast over a Havana radio station that could be heard in Miami. By listening closely one could hear the balls run down the chute and hear the judges call out both the number and the prize. They spoke Spanish, of course, but a smart "Cuba" player always listened for the three thuds of the judge's gavel that accompanied the big winners. Only the last two digits of the first top prize counted in Florida. Thus, if the first prize number in Havana was 17892, the numbers operators would pay at 70 to 1 odds all those who had bet on 92.

The big advantage of "Cuba" was the confidence it inspired in the suckers by virtue of the fact that the drawing was held in a foreign country and the results could be immediately ascertained by radio. It seemed unfixable. The big disadvantage, from the operator's viewpoint, was just that—it was unfixable. One could never be sure when a red-hot number would turn up and cost the operators a fortune. Numbers players play hunches. Any date such as Christmas or Labor Day or Lincoln's Birthday or one's own birthday is sufficiently suggestive to bring a bet. After all, they have to have

Bolita slip guides may easily be purchased at many New York newsstands.

Above, players in a policy shop in the 1890s, and left, a cartoon from the 1870s showing the indecision of a policy player.

some system for picking a number. When a lot of them bet on the same number, it becomes hot because the payoff would be huge if it turned up. Some numbers remain constantly popular, usually low ones, and are seldom allowed to win.

In the old days, when the syndicate was busy with other things, the independent numbers operators tried several times to put the fix in with Cuban President Batista. They were told that the Cuban National Lottery was sacred and could not be rigged—too much depended on public confidence in it. When Castro took office, he closed down the casinos but allowed the lottery to continue. After some months, word spread in Florida underworld circles that Castro was indeed rigging the lottery—but for the benefit of his own agents in Miami and Tampa. Armed in advance with knowledge of the winning number, they were able to spread a lot of bets around and were milking the operators dry. When this author wrote a story about it, Castro abruptly abolished the lottery, forcing the Florida racketeers to turn to other sources for their number.

Corruption has always been a way of life along the Gold Coast, and over the years authorities have blamed bolita and "Cuba" for much of it. The racket has always kept a low profile, getting little publicity. Police and prosecutors have usually been tolerant. The situation isn't unique to Florida, of course. Around the nation, numbers is the biggest source of lower-level graft in the country, surpassing bookie joints and prostitution.

Perhaps one of the most bizarre cases involving bolita was the disappearance of Judge and Mrs. Curtis Chillingworth from their home in Palm Beach, Florida, in 1955. Eventually they were declared legally dead, but for five years the mystery remained. Then, abruptly, a professional bagman and enforcer confessed, and fingered the handsome and highly respected former municipal judge, Joseph A. Peel, as the mastermind.

Investigation revealed that while in office Peel had collected graft from bolita operators as well as moonshiners on a regular basis. If

Opposite page, Joseph A. Peel, Jr.,
accused of masterminding the
killing of Judge and Mrs. C. E.
Chillingworth in 1961, is greeted by
his wife Imogene after being
questioned by the state's attorney.
Above and right, Judge and Mrs.
C. E. Chillingworth, victims of a
bizarre murder in June 1955,
thought to have been carried out to
avoid uncovering Peel's illegal
dealings in the numbers games.

any of them got arrested, he either dismissed the case on technicalities or subtracted the small fine from their graft payments. The man who squealed was one of his two partners who did the dirty work.

Chillingworth was a Superior Court judge in Palm Beach, and as such was scheduled to hear complaints against Judge Peel. Since Chillingworth was considered honest and unbribeable, Peel decided the only thing to do was kill him.

The two men he assigned the task did their work well—with only one complication. When they approached the Chillingworth home from the ocean that June night, they intended to take only the judge. But Mrs. Chillingworth came into the room to join her husband, and the men decided they had no choice if the murder was to remain a mystery.

The couple was taken a mile or two out to sea. Mrs. Chillingworth was weighed down and dropped over first. The judge managed to jump overboard and he tried to swim away despite the fact that his hands were tied behind his back. He was pursued, hit with a shotgun borrowed from Judge Peel, and weighed down with the boat's anchor. The bodies were never found.

The trial in 1961 attracted national attention, primarily because it concerned two judges and the lack of a *corpus delicti*. Very little was made of the fact that bolita was behind the whole case. One of the actual killers was given immunity in exchange for his testimony; the other pleaded guilty and became a state witness. Peel, exuding charm and mixing some truth with his lies, fought almost alone and was rewarded when the jury tempered its guilty verdict with a recommendation of mercy. That made life imprisonment a mandatory sentence.

There was another result not immediately apparent. The information about the profits from bolita attracted the attention of organized crime. Within two years the numbers action from Palm Beach south to the Keys was under the control of a giant man named Hyman "Fat Hymie" Martin. Back in the old days in Cleveland he had once been tried for murder and convicted—but he got a new trial and beat the rap. Among those working for Martin in 1965 was a man named Blount.

Top, Gunnar Myrdal, who made astute observations about the relationship between policy and organized crime, and above, Hyman Martin, one of the mobsters to cash in on the profits available in controlling games of bolita. Opposite page, an 1841 ticket for the Kentucky Literature Lottery.

Literature Lottery

BY AUTHORITY OF THE STATE OF KENTUCKY

Class No. **205** Com Nos. 10 48 75

This Ticket will entitle the holder to one QUARTER of such Prize as may be drawn to its Numbers, if demanded within twelve months after the Drawing: Subject to a deduction of Fifteen per cent.: Payable forty days after the Drawing.

For A. BASSFORD & CO, Managers.

Covington, 1841. QUARTER.

The numbers racket has been around a long time. Called "lottery policy" when it first appeared in London in the last half of the eighteenth century, the racket permitted a player who couldn't afford to buy a lottery ticket to bet that a number he selected would be drawn in the lottery.

Horace Walpole described the game in a letter to the Countess of Ossory on December 17, 1789, in this fashion:

"As folks in the country love to hear of London fashions, know, Madam, that the reigning one among the quality is to go, after the opera, to the lottery office, where their Ladyships bet with the keepers. You choose any number you please; if it does not come up next day, you pay five guineas; if it does, receive forty. . . ."

Gambling operators soon realized that lottery policy could exploit more than persons of quality. It became very popular with poor people and was brought to America with the lottery. A committee of the New York legislature reported that in 1818 a lottery office in New York City made a profit of $31,000 on lottery policy in just three days. By 1835 the name was shortened to "policy." The Kentucky Literature Lottery, a state-operated drawing for the benefit of higher education, was used for years to supply the winning New York number, and the Louisiana Lottery supplied one for southern bettors.

When lotteries fell into disfavor, other methods were used. W. E. B. Dubois described the workings of the racket in 1899 in his famous book, *The Philadelphia Negro.* Gunnar Myrdal, in his even more famous study, *An American Dilemma,* wrote in 1944:

"The policy game started in the Negro community and has a long history. During most of its history the policy racket in the Negro community has been monopolized by Negroes. Otherwise respectable businessmen have had a controlling interest in the numbers racket. . . . When bootlegging became less profitable, the organized white criminal gangs "muscled in" and not only took control of the numbers racket in the Negro community but introduced it into the white community where it now flourishes all over the United States. The New York investigation into the activities of "Dutch" Schultz, head of the numbers racket, revealed a close tie between his activities and those of the Tammany political machine."

Myrdal was, of course, correct in noting the relationship of the numbers racket to politics. Because it involves nickels, dimes, and quarters, it is easy for uninformed citizens to ignore. And in the absence of scrutiny, corrupt law-enforcement officials can get rich without great risk. When and if confronted with evidence, they can always follow the example of Judge Douglas Lambeth and declare, "A thousand men couldn't wipe out bolita." The public, not knowing much about it. is willing to accept such a verdict. Some experts say that numbers—call it policy or bolita—finances more corruption than any other illegal activity in America.

The man who perhaps more than any other was responsible for taking the numbers racket away from Negro bosses and making it available to poor whites as well was, interestingly enough, a Puerto Rican named Jose Enrique Miro. He came to the United States in 1927 by signing on as a stoker on a freighter, but once in New York, he buried himself in Harlem where his dark skin was not conspicuous. Quickly, he moved in on the numbers racket, not by force but by having an aptitude for numbers.

The racket in Harlem was based on three-digit numbers that paid off, in theory at least, at a rate of 600 to 1. Miro got his payoff number from daily newspaper accounts of business at the New York Clearing House—a reporting service for banks. The first two digits were obtained from totals of all bank closings on the day of play, with the formula calling for the last two digits in the thousands figure of the total. In other words, if the total was $9,525,913, the selected number would be 25. To that would be added the last digit in the thousands column of the preceding day. Thus, if it totaled $8,986,543, 6 would be taken, making the winning number 256.

While to the uneducated, this sounded honest enough, it was possible to manipulate the number to get the desired results with some help from a friendly banker and some juggling of bank accounts. With big money involved, this wasn't as difficult as it sounds. Miro had ten different bank accounts with hundreds of thousands of dollars in each. And in those days before the stock market crash of 1929, banking practices were rather informal and largely unregulated.

Arthur Flegenheimer, "Dutch Schultz," head of the numbers racket in New York during the early 1930s who amassed a sizable empire before being eliminated by members of the Syndicate who considered him to be too much competition. Opposite page, Otto "Abbadabba" Biederman, killed with Schultz in a Newark, N.J., restaurant. Schultz' empire was divided among the big boys in the Syndicate, the Cleveland Syndicate getting the racetrack near Cincinnati—the one whose races Schultz had used to "fix" the numbers racket payoff.

Miro's success, inevitably, attracted the attention of a bigger robber baron. Arthur Flegenheimer, better known as "Dutch" Schultz, was an empire builder on the make. Big in beer, he wanted new worlds to conquer. Instead of knocking off the Puerto Rican, however, he simply moved in on him, supplying new capital and muscle. Miro was allowed to keep one-fourth of the profits, and this enabled him to bank $283,427 in 1929 and $566,409 in 1930. Unhappily for him, he neglected to pay any income taxes on it.

Following the 1929 crash, which destroyed confidence in banks and brokers, Schultz introduced a new formula for obtaining the winning number. Aware that suckers keep playing the horses year after year, Schultz decided the pari-mutuel handle at a racetrack would inspire new faith in the numbers players. Each day the total was published on the sports pages for all to see, and from it the winning three-digit number was selected. The players didn't realize that the racetrack in question was owned by Dutch or some of his gangster pals, and that the Dutchman employed a financial wizard, a living computer named Otto "Abbadabba" Biederman, to rig the number each racing day.

Many years later the same system was in operation in the Boston area. The "wise guys" had thirty minutes from the time they stopped writing bets on the street before the betting windows at the track were closed. In that interval they decided which number was "coldest" and the pari-mutuel handle at the track was adjusted to reflect it. All of which proves that a good thing is worth imitating.

An Internal Revenue Bureau investigation of Miro uncovered much evidence of Tammany Hall involvement with Dutch Schultz and other racketeers. It coincided with a probe ordered by Governor Franklin D. Roosevelt and conducted by Judge Samuel Seabury. Miro was indicted and, with Assistant United States Attorney Thomas E. Dewey prosecuting, was convicted and sentenced to three years in prison. During the trial, evidence was presented that Miro kept Tammany leaders *and* Schultz supplied with silk shirts. When Dutch was asked about this, he made his classic reply:

"Only queers wear silk shirts."

Seabury's probe continued and led ultimately to Mayor James J. Walker, New York's still admired playboy-crook. Walker resigned. Schultz was indicted but managed to beat the rap. When he wanted to have Dewey "hit," his colleagues in the crime syndicate ordered him eliminated. On October 23, 1935, Schultz was blasted at the Palace Chop House in Newark. Three associates including Abbadabba were killed with him. The latter had just returned from Cincinnati where a racing meet had ended at the Coney Island Race Track—a track owned by Dutch.

The tough Schultz didn't die quickly. A police stenographer sat beside his bed in the hospital making note of every remark. Police found this comment puzzling:

"Please crack down on the Chinaman's friends and Hitler's commander. I am sore and I am going up and I'm going to give you honey if I can. Mother is the best bet and don't let Satan draw you too fast."

"Who shot you?" asked the stenographer.

"The boss," said Schultz." A few minutes later he was dead, and his ramblings remained largely a mystery.

Years passed before this author learned that "the Chinaman" was Louis Dalitz, brother of Moe Dalitz of the Cleveland syndicate. Louis was in the laundry business and had been known as Louis the Chinaman for many years. Anyone in the laundry business in those days ran the risk of being called by a similar nickname, so firmly had the Chinese become identified with the washing of clothes. And the Cleveland syndicate—the Chinaman's friends—was even then trying

Mayor Jimmy Walker being
questioned during Judge Samuel
Seabury's investigation into
corruption in New York in the
1930s. At left, Judge Seabury waits
for an answer.

Michael "Trigger Mike" Coppola and his wife Doris. Coppola, opposite page, controlled the numbers racket in New York during the 1940s.

to take the Coney Island Race Track from Dutch. They succeeded, renamed it River Downs, and operated it for many years. Other members of the developing national syndicate divided up Schultz's empire. Michael "Trigger Mike" Coppola got the Harlem numbers racket.

A native of Salerno, Italy, Coppola was brought to New York while still a baby. One of nine children, he finished the seventh grade before being listed an "incorrigible delinquent." By the age of twenty-five he had been in prison five times, including one thirty-month stretch in Sing Sing. With his apprenticeship behind him, the little man— only five feet, five inches tall—won wealth and a reputation during Prohibition, and gained a foothold in the numbers racket. When Schultz was killed, he was the logical man to take over for the syndicate.

Despite the much-celebrated "big heat" in New York, which saw such men as Luciano jailed and Louis Lepke executed, Coppola ruled his domain without incident. The public, as usual, was unconcerned with what appeared to be a nickel-and-dime racket centered among people of low income, and the press found it difficult to get information that might have revealed the true millionaire status of the business.

In 1946, however, the murder of Joseph Scottoriggio, a Republican precinct captain, caused a great deal of trouble for Trigger Mike. His wife was indicted for perjury when she lied to protect the mob. The former dancer died abruptly while giving birth to a daughter, and Coppola was off the hook. Nevertheless, he turned the racket over to his lieutenants and moved to Miami Beach. He returned at intervals to check up on operations, but for the most part he was content to rule by courier.

His second wife, the former Ann Drahmann of Cincinnati, has testified as to the profits of the business. There was the day, she said, when Mike came home from the Midtown Social Club where he had spent the afternoon playing cards with Joe Massei. In the middle of dinner, he suddenly clapped his hands to his face, cursed loudly in Italian, and rushed to the telephone. As Ann listened, he ordered the club manager to

Frank "Screw" Andrews, head of a Cincinnati numbers empire in the 1950s and owner of Newport, Kentucky, casinos.

find a package he had left in the freezer and to send the package to the Coppola home immediately.

A few minutes later a messenger from the club arrived with a fairly large package. Mike, who was eating calmly now, explained that a courier had brought the package to the club earlier in the day and he had placed it in the freezer for safekeeping. Then he had forgotten it was there.

After dinner, the Coppolas went upstairs to the bedroom and there Ann helped her husband count $219,000 in assorted bills. It was Mike's cut from the Harlem numbers racket for the final quarter of the year 1958.

"Not bad," said Trigger Mike.

He gave Ann ten thousand dollars of the total for a Christmas present.

But Mike's interest in numbers wasn't confined to New York. According to his wife, he was the financial backer of Frank "Screw" Andrews, the numbers boss of greater Cincinnati with headquarters in the Sportsman Club in downtown Newport, Kentucky.

Andrews was a tough, cold man, ruthless in his drive for wealth. With Coppola's money behind him, he bought protection in Newport and killed his way to power. For many years the numbers racket in the Cincinnati area had been left to Negro kingpins, the crime syndicate being too busy with its plush casinos. Screw killed the Negro leaders one by one, pleading self-defense when occasionally charged with murder, and he got away with it. By 1960 he was in complete control.

A citizens' revolt in Newport began in 1958 and reached a climax in 1961. Almost incidentally, Screw's numbers empire came under investigation along with casinos, bookie joints, and brothels. On July 18, 1961, a task force of IRS special agents broke down the doors of the Sportsman Club and surged inside. They found slot machines concealed on a pivot inside the wall, so delicately balanced that a slight touch would bring them swinging around and into play. They found a complicated device which used compressed air to blow numbered

Ping-Pong balls into the air until one of them fell into a chute and rolled free. This was Screw's version of bolita—the on-premise drawing of the winning number in full view of hundreds of spectators. Considerable study was necessary before the special agents learned how to operate the machine so that the desired number would pop out, but when they found the system, it was infallible.

Many hours passed, however, before the investigators found what they really wanted—Screw's records. They were stored in a hidden room. Entrance to the room was gained when an agent searching a closet came across a piece of wire some ten inches long. Insulation had been cut back at both ends. Examination revealed two nailheads in the back of the closet, shoulder high and eight inches apart. On impulse, the agent touched the ends of the wire to the nailheads. A buzzing sound, and then the back of the closet swung open to reveal the secret room. A study of the records it contained produced evidence to show that Andrews was reporting for tax purposes only one-seventh of his million-dollar numbers business. The evidence sent Andrews to prison.

Coppola, in Miami Beach, was too busy with his own problems to help Andrews. For Ann had squealed on him and provided evidence to send him to prison on tax-evasion charges. Then, after requesting that her body be cremated and the ashes dropped on Coppola's Miami Beach home, she killed herself.

But the numbers racket continues under new management and will continue so long as it represents a poor man's only excuse to hope.

Sex and gambling don't mix very well as a general rule, since the one seems to supplant the other, but over the years some madams have learned that casual gambling has value in a brothel. The author gained some insight into this a few years back while snooping around the dark and dirty streets of Newport, Kentucky.

The Flamingo Club in Newport, Kentucky, where gambling and sex were business partners.

In a one-block radius of the police station were a dozen or more brothels and bustout joints, dives you don't get out of unless you're busted financially. Since the cops and the politicians couldn't seem to see them, I decided to visit a few. A church layman went along to give the proper moral tone to the expedition—and, incidentally, protect me from a frame. In those days in Newport, a reporter took precautions—or bribes.

We entered the Harbor Bar down near the Ohio River. A small, narrow room, it featured a dozen stools at the bar and perhaps a couple of tables. The bartender, fat and dirty, was reading a copy of *True Detectives.* He shifted his eyes from the printed page long enough to glance at us and say, "The girls and the slots are upstairs."

At the end of the room we found a stairway. It creaked and groaned as we ascended, giving ample warning that two live ones were on their way up. At the top we stepped into a small sitting room. The bright colors were in garish contrast to the dingy bar below, but we had little opportunity to appreciate the improvement. Eight females assaulted us. Literally. They wore strips of fishnet across their breasts and other strips across their middles—it *was* the Harbor Bar—and they competed mightily to display their assets.

Later the madam came out and apologized. She had been involved with a disgruntled customer, she said, and the girls forgot themselves. After all, business was bad what with the grand jury meeting, and we did look like a couple of sports.

Be that as it may, as the girls pushed and clutched, I found myself turning instinctively to a row of slot machines that stood along a wall. Without waiting to see each score, I dropped in quarters and jerked the handle. The girls could only get to me from three sides, and that was some improvement.

A momentary respite came when the ancient one-armed bandit to which I was clinging, suddenly burbled and coughed up a handful of coins. They spilled on the floor. Instantly the girls went for them, shoving each other out of the way.

Later, after the madam appeared and calm

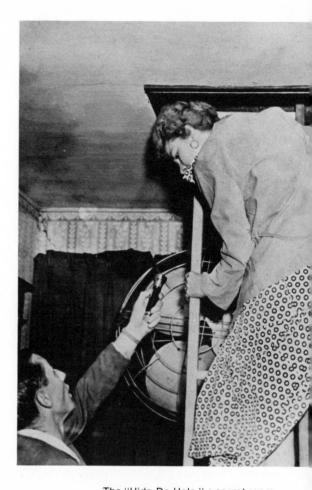

The "Hide-De-Hole," a secret room in the ceiling of the Hi-De-Ho Club in Newport, Kentucky. Opposite page, part of reporter Hank Messick's editorial essay on the wide open red light district in Newport, Kentucky, which thrives despite investigations.

developed, my friend and I accepted an invitation to sit down and "chat with the young ladies." We were discussing such mundane things as the price of "going French" when the stairs groaned and in came three college students. At least they looked like college students. The girls primly retained their seats and the youths headed for the slots. They played mechanically, glancing sideways at the bulging fishnets and talking in low voices to each other. It was then that I recognized that the slots provided a way for the inexperienced to feel sophisticated and slightly sinful while getting up courage for the real business of the evening. I had used the slots to buy time and that, essentially, was what the newcomers were doing.

In researching other joints in other cities, I found the same thing. Once when I congratulated a friendly madam about the psychology implicit in the use of the machines, she commented, "Yeah, and they make a pisspot full of money, too."

Slot machines have been making pisspots full of money for a varied lot of hustlers since Charles Fey, a young San Francisco mechanic, invented the first one in 1895. Instead of the familiar fruit symbols known today, Fey decorated his turning wheels with hearts, spades, and diamonds. Offsetting these rather common denominators were replicas of the Liberty Bell, complete with crack. And, logically enough, the biggest payoff—ten nickels—came on the bells. Why, a man could almost feel patriotic when three bells lined themselves up, and gamblers are always eager to appear patriotic.

Fey not only invented the machine and manufactured it by the thousands, he was also the first slot-machine operator. He gave himself the first franchise, so to speak, and placed hundreds of them in area bars and gambling joints on a fifty-fifty basis. Aware that he had a good thing, he refused to sell manufacturing rights to anyone else as the demand grew faster than he could supply

The Liberty Bell, the first one-armed bandit, built by Charles Fey in 1889. Opposite, his grandson, Marshall Fey, in Reno, Nevada.

it. Inevitably, a rival appeared. Herbert Mills of Chicago came up with a similar machine in principle but having enough differences in design to meet legal requirements. For instance, it carried an assortment of bells, bars, lemons, cherries, and the like, but no hearts, spades, or diamonds. By 1907 Mills was producing machines, and within a very few years, they were all over the country. Mills was many times a millionaire, and rival slot-machine operators were fighting bloody wars for control of a given territory.

The manner in which the slot machines proliferated is illustrated by the saga of Howard Vice. A tall, tough young man in 1917, Vice was trying to make a living in Newport, Kentucky. He and a pal, Charles Kroger, noticed an advertisement for one of Mills's machines in a magazine one day. It offered a chance to get rich quick, so the young men pooled their funds and ordered one from Chicago. After many hours of concentration, they learned how to get money out of the back, and finally, when they knew more about it than the potential suckers, they placed it in a candy store. It earned sixty dollars a week. Delighted, they moved it to a "beer camp" and people literally fought to play it.

There were problems, however. The machine kept breaking down. Weeks would pass before replacement parts could be obtained from Chicago. The youths got tired of their toy and sold it to Lawrence McDonough and "Boots" Ortlieb. These two older men, with more capital to invest, bought additional machines. They set up a route and hired a combination collector-repairman to attend to it. The hired hand soon stole enough from the machines to buy into the firm, and the first slot-machine syndicate in the area was born.

Ten years after Vice and Kroger brought the first slot machine to Campbell County, the grand jury on March 24, 1927, reported:

"The citizens of our county do not realize the magnitude of slot machine gambling. The daily income averages $8 per machine. It is estimated that about 150 machines are in operation. This means about half a million dollars per year. The tremendous possibilities of corruption are plainly seen."

A year later, another grand jury viewed the situation with alarm. It noted that "testimony brought before us has shown that men have squandered their weekly wages in just a short while in these machines."

The jury told the citizens that various mayors and police chiefs in the county had promised

Examples of slot machines from a trade publication of 1935.

"to order slot machines out immediately." Among those cited as promising a cleanup were Chief Frank Ortlieb of Dayton, the father of "Boots," and Chief Frank Bregal of Newport, whose son headed a rival syndicate.

It was 1952 before anything effective was done about the slot machines. In that year the FBI, acting under a new federal law, seized 1,432 slots in the Newport area and still missed a lot of them. Some legal tricks were necessary, but eventually the owners got them back. With the federal heat on, however, most of the machines stayed stored in a warehouse until 1960. When England legalized gambling at about that time, the owners discovered it was legally possible to ship the dusty machines abroad if a buyer could be found. That posed no problem, since the new British casinos were in large part controlled by American mobsters. A local crating company was hired to bundle up the ancient machines for shipment. Unhappily for the boys, some sneaky reformers managed to mislabel the crates. Tipped off, the FBI again seized the machines—this time on a New York dock. Again they went into a warehouse and, presumably, are still there. Collecting rust, of course, not silver.

As to Kroger and Vice—well, Kroger "fell"

out of a moving car a few years later following a dispute over bootleg profits. Vice made quite a reputation for himself as a tough bootlegger and bodyguard, but eventually he was framed on a murder charge. After many years in prison he settled down in an old house on a bluff high above the Ohio between Cincinnati and Louisville. Despite several chances, he had failed to hit the financial jackpot, but he had survived. Somehow that seemed a small accomplishment until he removed his shirt one day and showed me the scars of old bullet wounds. Then I understood.

In some respects, Vice's life resembled that of a slot-machine player. In most gambling games there is at least the hope that if one keeps doubling his bets and has patience and cash enough to keep playing, he can recover his losses when at last the odds make him a momentary winner. Not so with slots where the bet remains the same. Ultimately, if the player is patient, he will get a winning combination, but the payoff won't begin to cover the total loss. Thus, to be able to play a long time is a victory of a sort, and Vice looked upon life in the same way.

It is, of course, a fact that slot machines can

Slot machines came in a wide variety of novel styles and shapes. The barrel below dispensed beer. Above, a punchboard, another way to part people from their money. The owner of the store was usually told which hole had the winning slip when he purchased one and he would punch that hole, before the suckers could.

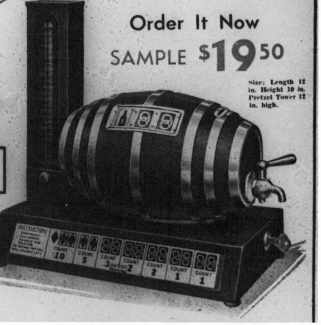

SPARK PLUG

Automatic Mystery Payout

MOST SENSATIONAL Race Horse Counter Game ever made! SPARK-PLUG needs only about 1 SQUARE FOOT counter space, runs 125 races an hour, takes in $50 to $100 a day! Simple, cheat-proof, trouble-proof. NON-ELECTRIC mechanism.

LATEST IMPROVED MODELS

Only **$29.50** Each

NATURAL

Actually 3 Games in One!

At last! A really new idea in a DICE GAME! NATURAL really gives you 3 distinct games, insuring TRIPLE PLAYER APPEAL and at least 3 TIMES LONGER LIFE ON LOCATION! In addition to 3 different games, you get 5 different fronts— for CIGARETTES, BEER and TRADE AWARDS! Needs only about 1 SQ. FT. space, takes in 3 to 4 nickels a minute! Get started with this busy little money maker today!

Only **$18.50** Each

ON THE WAY!
GALLOPING GHOST
(—AND—)
A COUNTER LITE-A-LINE
MARBLO
Modernistic . . . Twin Balls . . . Exciting!

MARBLO

NOW IN PRODUCTION ON
SYNCHRO
SAMPLES ON DISPLAY
AT ALL JOBBERS

DROP KICK

**HORSE
SHOES**
All the Bets
and
Thrills of a Real
HORSE RACE
The Prince
of counter games

*A Real
Football
Game*

SELECT-EM The Prince of counter games

Games dispensed surprises, cigarettes or beer—but very rarely the winning number. Sports have always been a popular theme in gambling, as can be seen here.

New York Mayor Fiorello La
Guardia is shown pursuing one of
his favorite sports, smashing over
$200,000 worth of slot machines.
Opposite page, Frank Costello, who
inherited Lucky Luciano's job on
his enforced departure for his
homeland. Costello controlled the
entire slot machine empire and ran
criminal activities in Louisiana as
well as along the Eastern Seaboard.

be preset to determine the amount of the payoff that led to the nickname "one-armed bandits." Some authorities credit Westbrook Pegler with coining the term. Gamblers, however, prefer a more romantic origin. They tell of two bank robbers—possibly John Dillinger and "Pretty Boy" Floyd—playing a slot machine in a midwestern hangout. Dillinger, who was dropping in the quarters, commented:

"You sure don't need no gun to rob somebody if you've got one of these things for him to play."

"Yep," replied Floyd, who was pulling the handle, "and this bandit has only one arm."

Whatever the origin, Las Vegas operators who believe patience can be encouraged by novelty, once built slot machines into the bodies of life-size, cast-iron figures of one-armed western outlaws. The one arm, of course, terminated in a slot-machine handle, allowing the sucker to play the machine by "shaking hands" with the bandit. As a gimmick, it was something to talk about back home in Fort Lauderdale, but the regular slots drew the more patient customers. To please them the operations created "Frankenstein," a bank of four machines bolted together with only one handle, which meant that four machines could be played with one-fourth the physical labor.

Patience, that quality praised by the Las Vegas operators, has always been a virtue possessed by the supermen of crime. Frank Costello was no exception, and his adventures with slot machines make an interesting commentary on the politics and politicians of the thirties.

The New York mob, flush with bootleg profits and in need of long-term investments, became interested in slot machines as early as 1929. That, at least, is the date given by Costello in public testimony. The Mills Company was the supplier, and in short order thousands of machines were installed throughout New York.

Huey P. Long whose winning streak ran out when he became overly ambitious and bucked Roosevelt's Administration in an attempt to succeed him in the White House. Costello spent $100,000 to legalize slot machines in Long's state of Louisiana. The machines earned double that amount in their first year of operation.

Since gambling per se was illegal, the hoods and the manufacturers combined to devise an acceptable gimmick. The machines were so constructed that, by inserting or removing a single cotter pin, the payoff could be changed from coins to candy mints and back again. The Tru-Mint Company was then formed. From an obliging judge it obtained an injunction prohibiting New York police from interfering with the versatile devices. A gentleman with the innocent-sounding name of Cecil J. Crabtree was listed as manager of the mint company, but the real executive was the remarkable "Dandy Phil" Kastel, who would later front for Costello in Las Vegas.

All went well for a while. Costello's profits were estimated to have reached $700,000 a week, and the figure is plausible. But action breeds reaction and, inevitably, reform sentiment came. Fiorello LaGuardia campaigned for mayor with religious intensity, and on January 1, 1934, he took office.

For Costello and his Mafia associates, "the Little Flower," as LaGuardia was known, was bad news. Of Italian descent, he was a popular hero to millions of Italian-Americans. The usual smear along ethnic lines wouldn't work. Violence was unthinkable. And since the man wouldn't be bribed, he was almost untouchable.

The crusade launched one minute after LaGuardia took office wasn't always effective, but it was spectacular. Ironically, various civil liberties groups took exception as the mayor ordered his cops to fight fire with fire. Among other things they began confiscating Costello's slot machines. With every indication of pleasure, the chubby LaGuardia personally supervised the deep-sixing of them in the Atlantic Ocean.

Costello's legal wizards screamed in protest, citing the hitherto sacred injunction. Undeterred, the cops kept rounding up the machines. Costello ordered the remainder into hiding. Now was the time for patience. And sure enough, opportunity in the form of Huey Long, the kingfish of Louisiana, came to town and got involved in a squabble in the men's room of a leading hotel.

One of the Italian street festivals in New York City, this one in honor of St. Anthony of Padua. Below, some of the gaming devices that always play a large part in such festivals.

A Franciscan friar decorates a statue of St. Anthony with currency. Below, another friar tries his luck. Opposite page, large wheels and layouts inside the church where more expensive bets can be placed.

Costello's men rescued him, and Costello soothed his feelings, plied him with good liquor, and made him a proposition. As eager for a fast buck as anyone else, Long accepted. The New York slots would go south for the political winter.

Peter Hand, a New Orleans hustler and political hack, ended up with a small percentage of the slot machines. His unpublished memoirs are quite revealing.

The slots took in some $800,000 in about six months. Long's cut was $20,000 a month. He picked it up from a box in the Roosevelt Hotel. Charitable enterprises, in whose names the entire operation was functioning, received a grand total of $600. The rest of the money was divided among the operators of the various bars, candy stores, and clubs where the slots were placed, and the New York syndicate, which included, in addition to Costello and Kastel, such enterprising individuals as Meyer Lansky.

Matters became complicated on September 8, 1935, when Long was fatally shot. That meant his political heirs had to be cut in, and a conference at Hot Springs, Arkansas with Owney "the Killer" Madden presiding as host was necessary. But there was enough loot to go around, and soon the slots were feeding again.

Another shakeup came in 1940 when it was necessary to organize the Louisiana Mint Company to sponsor the machines. It was the old dodge—candy for sure, coins once in a while—and it worked. Hand's ten percent was worth $3,500 a month "or better," he said. That, of course, was after payoffs to city and county officials, made necessary by changing political conditions and the lack of a strong "boss." But still things worked well enough. Independents were permitted to own six machines each. If anyone put out more than six, the police raided them.

At one point, Hand reports, he suggested to Kastel that they get the slots legalized, "but he was deathly afraid of that, thinking somebody else would put out too many of them." Legalized slots could have been achieved at a cost of only two hundred dollars per vote in the legislature, Hand said.

Kastel was shortsighted in deciding to keep

Opposite page, children in the area of the street fair imitate their elders. The object of their game is to drop coins through a slot in the larger jar and get them into a smaller jar floating in the water inside. Above, Mayor deLesseps Morrison of New Orleans, who cleaned the slot machines out of his city in 1946.

things illegal. In 1946, Mayor deLesseps Morrison took office and ran the slots out of town. Many of them simply crossed the river to the dives of Gretna in Jefferson Parish, where they continued to operate for another two decades. Kastel moved on to Las Vegas where slots—and everything else—were legal.

Perhaps because of Costello's reputation, slot machines have always been a little less respectable than, say, roulette, which suggests a sophisticated, slightly Continental aura. When the "New World Riviera," as the P.R. flacks called it, opened on Grand Bahama in 1964, there was much publicity about the *lack* of slot machines. None of that vulgar Las Vegas flavor would be tolerated. Within three months there were thousands of machines. More recently, Puerto Rico announced that to stimulate sagging business in its recession-ridden casinos, slot machines would be added for the first time.

All of which brings to mind the story of the drunk who played a one-armed bandit for hours in one of the downtown Las Vegas slot-machine jungles. As he dropped in quarters, he sipped from a pocket flask. Finally, with both pockets and flask empty, he rushed from the building to return a minute later with a tire iron. Savagely he assaulted the slot-machine that had robbed him. Other frustrated players gathered around and cheered him on. It looked like a revolt was brewing.

The manager, aided by a uniformed cop, intervened to save the slot machine while it was still functional. As the cop wrestled away the tire iron, the manager wagged his finger jovially at the crowd.

"You have to have faith," he said. Stepping forward, he dropped another coin in the machine. What else he did, if anything, no one could be sure, but, abruptly, a fountain of quarters gushed forth.

"See what I mean," said the manager.

"Jackpot."

The drunk, shaking his head in disbelief, was led outside by the cop and turned loose, and the spectators, faith restored, rushed back to their own machines.

It is amusing to speculate what would happen to Las Vegas if at a given moment a sizable number of slot-machine addicts regained their sanity and rebelled. Glitter Gulch might look like Havana on the evening of January 1, 1959, after Batista and Lansky fled. The happy crowds celebrated by breaking slot machines.

One-armed bandits take a crushing defeat under the tracks of a tank in Baumholder, West Germany, where they were removed from a United States Army Noncommissioned Officers Club in 1972.

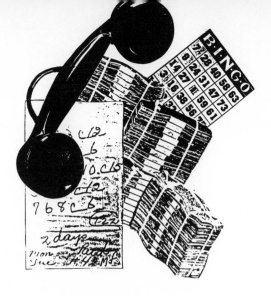

5 THE BASIC BOOKIE

The raiders were divided into two parties. One headed north for Miami Shores and the home of John "the Greek" Prokos. I accompanied the other group led by Assistant Attorney General Ed Cowart to downtown Miami and the huge but half-empty Langford Building. Months before, I had visited that building and written a news story about the unique bookie operation it housed. Now I would have a chance to check the accuracy of my information.

Cowart remained in his car, in touch with both raiding parties by radio. Chief investigator Jim McCall led us into the building just at dusk. The elevator man, an employee of Prokos, refused to let us off on the fourth floor. No one, he said firmly, was permitted on the fourth floor after 6 P.M. McCall gave an order; the man was placed under arrest. We got off at the fourth floor.

The hall space was limited and gave access to only four doors. We knocked at room 420, which bore the name "Factory Planning Service." No one replied. McCall gestured. A sledgehammer thudded against the door panel, splintering it. We rushed into the room. It was empty.

Empty of humans, that is, but on a table sat a telephone and an open briefcase. Inside the briefcase was a mass of electronic equipment. Even as we looked the telephone rang softly, lights inside the briefcase glowed brightly, and there was a clicking sound. The telephone call was being transferred automatically to Prokos's home some ten miles away in the suburbs.

The device was known as a "cheesebox" because the first one discovered by law-enforcement officials had been hidden in a cheesebox. Or so went the legend. At any rate, it was compact and efficient. To move it, one needed only to unhook the wires leading to the phone, close the briefcase, and walk away like any other respectable investment counselor. (Bookies, when they pass to that great crap game in the sky are often called "investment counselors" in their newspaper obits.)

Part of the setup was the adjoining room. During daylight hours, Prokos's people sometimes worked there while the machine next door diverted calls to them. The name of a dress designer was on the door, but we broke in anyway. Inside was only a telephone, a dress pattern, and a knife.

Hastily we took the elevator to the ninth floor where we again crashed through two doors to find the same arrangements: In one room an active cheesebox diverting calls to Prokos's home, and in the next a silent telephone.

Triumphant, we passed the word to Cowart who ordered the second raiding party into action. Within minutes the raiders were inside

Two detectives take over a Chicago
bookie's wire room and continue to
answer the phone and take bets.
Opposite page, a cheesebox
switching device which supplied
bettors with telephone numbers
they could call to place bets. It
allowed the bookie to be
somewhere else which was helpful
in case of a raid.

the house. Prokos ran to the bathroom to flush betting slips down the toilet, but it hardly mattered. Officers manned his telephone and began accepting the bets still being relayed from the Langford Building downtown. Among them was a five-thousand-dollar bet on a night baseball game.

Prokos was dressed in a softball uniform when arrested. The stocky, dark-haired veteran explained he was on a neighborhood team and was scheduled to play that night— after all, the bets were in on the pros, of course. With his brother, Chris, he had been booking bets in downtown Miami for many years. They operated a Greek restaurant, and, in the past, had used it as a front for accepting bets in the traditional fashion. Things had changed, however, when Attorney General Robert Kennedy sponsored legislation that almost destroyed the bookie business. New techniques had been needed to circumvent the new laws, and the cheese-box was one such technique.

In brief, it permitted the bookie to supply his regular customers with several telephone numbers. Anytime they wanted to take a shot at something, be it ball game, horse race, or fight, they called and identified themselves with a prearranged code number. The bet was then taken. Every month or so, the wins and losses were added up, and the customer billed accordingly. It was all very efficient. If, however, someone talked and police or some federal agency learned the telephone numbers used, the cheesebox offered security. The cops might trace the number to its address, get a warrant, and bust in. All they would find would be a telephone. The bookie taking the action might be in the next room or miles away.

Of course, in Miami in those days it took tremendous heat to persuade state and local law-enforcement officials into action, but Prokos believed in taking precautions. These had failed only because the raiders had learned about the cheeseboxes and had search warrants for both ends of the operation. The attorney general, it should be added, was up for reelection and had to do

A chariot race decorating a Greek
Sixth-century B.C. krater.

something dramatic to restore his image as a crime-buster.

You might say Prokos was the victim of politics. Fair enough, you might add, since politics had made his long career possible in the first place.

Bookies and politicians have been playing games with each other since man tamed the horse. Cylinders have been found dating back at least to 4000 B.C. which show warriors using horse-drawn chariots in battle. And chariot racing didn't begin with Ben Hur. It is safe to assume, human nature being little changed, that the old argument as to the fastest horse began immediately. It is equally safe to assume that the proud owners wagered worldly goods on their favorite animals. A third assumption is equally valid — as soon as betting became general, the bookie made his appearance to offer odds and accept bets from other interested parties. Racing and betting go together, as was illustrated for the author some years ago in a meadow outside Louisville.

As a new reporter for *The Courier-Journal*, I had been given the routine task of checking out several reports of illegal handbook activity in the vicinity of Churchill Downs. In my innocence, I took the assignment seriously and penetrated several well-established books. Louisville, I discovered,

was littered with bookie joints. At one intersection, I found books on three of the four corners, and all appeared to be doing a steady business. It was during this investigation that I became sick of beer. Protocol demanded you buy a mug in the saloon outside before venturing into the backroom. I learned to visit the toilet and pour the stuff out. Eventually, of course, the bookies got on to me, and when police reluctantly moved into action they found my picture pasted beside the peephole of one large handbook.

After a steady diet of handbooks, it was a relief one Saturday to be assigned to do a color story on the annual Oxmoor Steeplechase. Basically, it was a social event — the sons and daughters of the River Road elite, the "horsy set," turning out en masse to demonstrate their skills and the skills of their prize animals by jumping over various artificial barriers on the farm known as Oxmoor. For their parents, a small grandstand was set up and fenced off to keep out the common herd.

I was enjoying the lovely weather and the fact that it wasn't necessary to buy beer when suddenly I spotted a man in a dark suit wandering through the fenced-in area. He had money in his hands, and people kept coming up to him. I followed suit, and in a friendly chat learned that the guy was an

Top, a chariot race from a first
century B.C. Roman terra-cotta
relief, and above, a depiction of one
of the many racing games favored
by the American Indians.

Top, this race scene adorns the hope chest of a Florentine bride in celebration of her wedding in 1417. Above, English governor Richard Nichols (with cane) established the first American racecourse on Hempstead Plain in 1655 on the present site of Belmont Park, New York.

Above, one of the much publicized races between the Northern-bred champion, Fashion, and her equally matched opponent from the South, Peytona. On May 15, 1845, in the last of the epic races at the Union Course on Long Island, New York, Peytona defeated Fashion twice. However, in every later race between the two mares, Fashion was the winner. Left, racing at Jerome Park in 1867, one of the New York tracks established by financier Leonard W. Jerome, founder of the New York Jockey Club and grandfather of Sir Winston Churchill.

imported bookie, brought in just to handle the action at the Oxmoor. It had become a tradition, he said, and he enjoyed it very much.

Being a hardheaded reporter, I called over the photographer assigned to the event and told him to get an action shot of the bookie. The weekend city editor wasn't too excited about my story of open gambling at Oxmoor, but I pointed out that if we printed stories about workingmen's bookie joints we ought to give the same treatment to wealthy sports. The story ran with a picture.

I wasn't exactly rebuked the following Monday, but I was told to forget about bookies for a while. A year passed, and again it was time for Oxmoor. Alan Levy, who was later to become a popular writer for *Life* magazine and an author of several books, got the assignment. He was told to forget about gambling and concentrate on the pretty girls and the high-jumping horses. Alan returned somewhat amused. The bookie, he said, had been there as usual and this time he had been arrested. The cops, naturally figuring that if the newspaper that they considered the voice of the Establishment had objected the year before, they should do something this year. Since an arrest had been made, *The Courier-Journal* thought it necessary to write a little story. It was all very embarrassing.

Next year the problem was solved. The Oxmoor Steeplechase wasn't covered by the press. If there was any gambling there, the paper knew nothing of it. By then I had been assigned to cover Newport, a hundred miles away, where gambling was—frightful thought—controlled by an outside syndicate. Everything is relative. Later I was to learn that a friendly neighborhood bookie in Louisville would be a "Capone lieutenant" in Chicago, that a two-bit hoodlum in Miami would be a "boss of all the bosses" in New York, that a gangster anywhere could be a "philanthropist" on Miami Beach.

The first known public exhibition of horse racing was in Egypt in 1500 B.C. Chariot racing became an event of the Olympic games in 680 B.C. With nationalism a strong emotion, it is safe to say that bookies

Dissemination of racing news to betting parlors direct from the track was barred at one time in New York, but various ways were found to let bettors know how the race was going. Signals ranged from waving a fan or handkerchief and raising an umbrella (opposite page) to sitting on a watchtower. The information was then relayed to a telegrapher outside the track.

were busy figuring odds and accepting bets from those anxious to uphold the honor of Athens or Sparta.

Skipping over the Dark Ages, one finds horse racing and gambling in England in the twelfth century, but it wasn't until 1780 that the Earl of Derby originated the first horse racing event on a sweepstakes basis. That event is still held—the Epsom Derby. The sport crossed the English Channel during the long reign of Louis IV, "Le Roi Soleil," who also built the palace of Versailles, and it was in France a century later that the pari-mutuel machine was born.

Before that happened, however, racing crossed the Atlantic. Governor Richard Nichols of New York, disturbed by the lack of horses fit for a gentleman, created the first track on Long Island not far from the present location of Belmont Park. It was to be a testing ground, a means of selecting the better horses and thus improving the breed. Generations of gamblers since have insisted that the real interest in racing remains the improvement of the breed—the excitement and wagering is only incidental. To the uninitiated it would seem that if any breed is in urgent need of improvement it would be man not horses, but such cynics obviously lack sporting blood.

Gradually, the "auction pool" system of betting evolved and became the recognized way of doing it. The auctioneer assembled a group of sports and offered each horse in turn. Those who believed that Ancient Age was the most likely to win bid for the honor of holding the ticket. The high bid got that honor. Then the process was repeated with the second horse, and so on down the line. Say five horses were entered in the race and the total of the high bids for each horse was $1,650. The man who played the favorite risked the most, of course, with the man who bid on the horse considered least likely to succeed risking the smallest amount. The race was run and Ancient Age came through as expected. The holder of the high bid won the combined total bet on the race, minus, of course, five percent or $82.50 to the auctioneer and the $500 he bid. Even so, he was $1,067.50 ahead. But if Jack Daniels surprised everyone, the sport who risked only $100 on him won $1,467.50 in profits.

In 1933 electronic totalizers, such as this one in Arlington Park, Chicago (top), were installed for the first time at race courses throughout the country. Horse racing was legal in sixteen states in that year.

The auctioneer didn't stop with one pool, of course. As soon as he finished with one group, he turned to another. A man with a fixed conviction could risk his money a dozen times, and, of course, many did. Even so, the betting procedure was limited to a small class. There was little opportunity for the rank and file—the man known today as the $2 bettor. Of course, such a person could bet with another if he wanted to, but essentially the sport was considered the province of the aristocrat.

Refinements were added. The men who had bet on the horses coming in second and third were allowed smaller shares of the pool. This led to today's place and show betting. When a number of horses were entered and too many lacked fans willing to bid, the auctioneer permitted several to be bid upon as a group. This led to today's field betting.

Inevitably, with interest growing and more money being wagered, crooked dealings increased. Many an auctioneer became a bookie, accepting cash bets from the general public. The percentage charged for the service increased from five to twenty, and rumors circulated of fixed races and other monkey business. More and more tracks came into existence and the bookies paid a fixed fee for the privilege of operating at a track. The system was much like the imported bookie at Oxmoor. Bettors could shop around to find the bookie offering the best odds. It became common practice for a bookie to bribe a jockey to lose a race he was supposed to win. The bookie in the know had various ways of winning big, even if he had to cheat his fellow bookie to do it.

In an effort to end the domination of the sport by the bookies and to keep some of the betting profits for the track, Pierre Oller in France in 1865 invented the pari-mutuel machine. It enabled the owner of the machine, be he the track operator or a book licensed to take bets, to make money on every race regardless of which horse won.

In 1875 Lewis M. Clark organized the Louisville Jockey Club which held its first meeting at Churchill Downs. One of their feature races that year was a one-and-a-half mile dash for three-year-olds. Known as the Kentucky Derby, it has been renewed every year since.

Colonel Matt Winn, Clark's successor, made the Kentucky Derby the most sought-after race in America and was present himself at every one of its first seventy-five races. His keen business sense and flair for publicity led him to associations with racetracks throughout the United States and Mexico.

Its basic premise was simple—tickets are sold on each horse and the payoff price of the winning ticket is decided by the amount bet on the winner in proportion to the amount bet on all the other nags in the race. Thus, a heavily bet favorite would pay only a few cents on the dollar, but a long shot getting few bets would pay off handsomely.

This principle guaranteed the future of racing, since it offered the chance of the big payoff, the jackpot, that every man dreams about. Bookies didn't like it, however, since it made their services obsolete. When Lewis M. Clark, founder of the Kentucky Derby at Churchill Downs, installed four of the "French Clicker Machines"—as Oller's invention was then known—for the first running of the Derby, the bookies protested loudly. It took them fifteen years, but in 1890 they were powerful enough to force the Kentucky Jockey Club to stop using the machines. In the next eighteen years, the operations of the bookies became a scandal, and the Kentucky legislature passed antigambling laws. The thirty-fourth running of the Derby in 1908 was threatened until Colonel Matt Winn, Clark's successor at Churchill Downs, found six of the old Clickers stored in a barn. He had them renovated and put into service, bypassing the law which had been aimed at bookies. Stone Street galloped home, and the $5 mutuel tickets—the only price sold—paid $123.60 to win, $37.90 to place, and $14.50 to show.

Similar reaction to bookie-bred scandal caused reform movements in other states. New York passed an antigambling law in June 1908 that stopped horse racing in that state until pari-mutuels could be installed. New York City reformers went still further— they banned smoking by women in public places.

Technical advances continued with the development of automatic ticketing machines and the electric totalisator. It was now possible for the pari-mutuel clerk to accept a bet, press one button, and have the ticket printed and, at the same time, register the amount of the bet and other pertinent information with the totalisator. At ninety-second intervals, the total of new bets is added to the old and the odds are computed for individual races and flashed on "tote boards" in the infield, the clubhouse, and other convenient spots.

Betting slips from a bookie raid. Top, collectors or runners slips on which amounts wagered by the players are recorded. Known as the ''work,'' these slips are forwarded to the controller by pickup men. Right, New Jersey sheets.

Above, Charles Comiskey, the "Old Roman" who founded the Chicago White Sox and owned them for over thirty years. Opposite page, cartoons depicting the press reaction to the 1919 World Series when the scandal broke.

All of which made it possible for a lot of people to make bets on horse races at the track, and since not all horse players could take every afternoon off to go to the track, the bookies of America found themselves enjoying a new popularity and continuing prosperity. The player could console himself with the seeming illogic of a system that made betting at the track legal and betting outside the track illegal. The answer that at the track the profits were split with the state for various good causes didn't make much moral sense.

Gambling breeds gamblers, of course, and soon Americans were eager to bet on baseball games, fights, and election results. The bookie was ready to oblige, and the betting business grew rapidly. As always, the professional gambler was looking for a sure thing, and if a ball game could be fixed or the heavyweight champion persuaded to take a dive, the inclination was to do it.

Arnold Rothstein, a pioneer in many fields of organized crime, was basically a gambler and is best remembered today for fixing the 1919 World Series.

The Chicago White Sox team of 1919, owned by the "Old Roman," Charles Comiskey, was generally considered one of the best teams in baseball history. But they were unhappy. In many respects they resembled the world champion Oakland team of 1974. Comiskey was the Charley Finley of his day, and he believed in paying his players as little as possible. Many of his stars were paid the big-league minimum of $2,500. In the middle of the season, the players demanded raises. Comiskey, who reasoned the players either played for him or they didn't play, thanks to the famous reserve clause, said "No." Unhappy as they were, the players kept winning. They clinched the pennant early and had plenty of time to think about the World Series.

The Cincinnati Reds was a journeyman team, solid but not sensational. No one expected much of them, and when they won the National League pennant the bookies immediately established them as 4-to-1

"Step Lively"

—From The Philadelphia Evening Ledger

Just When Your Favorite Fruit Is Right

—From The Indianapolis News

underdogs. It was a perfect setup for a betting coup.

First to see the possibility were the unhappy, underpaid White Sox players. Here, they reasoned, was a chance to get those raises Comiskey had denied. It was true they had to play for the Old Roman, but they didn't have to play well.

Eddie Cicotte, the leading pitcher, was the ringleader. His major ally was first baseman Chick Gandhil. The two men approached Joe Sullivan, New England's biggest gambler. He liked the idea *but* said he couldn't provide the $100,000 bribe—$10,000 for ten players in on the scheme. He promised to talk to Rothstein and get the money.

Cicotte and Gandhil considered the deal complete, and proceeded to sound out their colleagues. Eventually, eight players were indicted, including five regular starters, the team's two best pitchers, and a utility infielder. One of the conspirators, "Shoeless Joe" Jackson, was considered second only to Ty Cobb as a hitter.

Rothstein took pains not to appear involved even to the players. He used Abe Attell, former featherweight champion of the world, as his front man. Attell moved into the Sinton Hotel with a coterie of twenty-five New York gamblers and began taking all bets on the first game in Cincinnati. As planned, the White Sox dropped the first game. A visitor to Attell's suite the next day said he looked about and saw "stacks of bills on every horizontal plane of the suite, except the ceiling. Dresser-tops, tables, and chair seats held yellow-backs. Mr. Attell, buried in currency, was perspiring with prosperity and behaving like a farm hand making love in a hay stack."

Yet Attell refused to pay the first installment of twenty thousand dollars, due after each losing game. He claimed he needed the cash to bet with. The White Sox, although disgruntled at finding gamblers as stingy as owners, kept their word and lost the second game. Still no payoff. Angry now, the team went out and won the third game. Attell took the hint and paid off. The White Sox lost the series, although it wasn't easy. Ironically, some of the players not in the know responded to the challenge and played the best ball of their lives to compensate for the strange errors their teammates were making.

Ban Johnson, president of the American League, heard rumors of a fix and hired private detectives to investigate. Almost a year later, he announced categorically that the White Sox had thrown the Series and that the man responsible was Arnold Rothstein. A grand jury investigation followed, indictments were returned, but in the interval before trial the evidence disappeared and the witnesses either vanished or recanted. The case was dismissed. Fearing the scandal would ruin baseball, however, the owners brought in Judge Kenesaw Mountain Landis to become the first commissioner of baseball and to police the business. Nothing was done about the reserve clause, however, and it wasn't until 1974 that Catfish Hunter revolted against Finley and got himself declared a free agent. Eight other teams offered him the millions Finley had refused, and Hunter signed with the New York Yankees.

Ironically, Rothstein had played it cautious— seemingly because he had difficulty believing the Series could be fixed. As a result, he won only $350,000 when, with more confidence, he might easily have made a million. But baseball was the national sport, and apparently even the cynical Rothstein was shocked. Out of the disillusionment occasioned by the 1919 World Series grew an adage that even today has much validity:

"Don't bet on anything that can talk."

Top, Ban Johnson, president of the American League, held an investigation that revealed the 1919 World Series had been fixed. Above, Judge Kenesaw Mountain Landis was engaged as the first baseball commissioner to insure that the scandal would not be repeated.

Horses, of course, couldn't talk, although tipsters were always reporting the latest data from the horse's mouth. In the wild decade before the Crash, millions of horse-players were cultivated. In an age of ballyhoo, of easy come and easier go, of disrespect for law and old standards of morality, gambling grew like Babe Ruth's ego. The Great Depression put a damper on things, but there was still the urge to bet, the hope that this time luck would smile and Daddy could buy baby that new pair of shoes she needed so badly.

The demand created new services. Racing forms came into general use, and horse players from coast to coast studied them for data on past performances, bloodlines, and the private lives of jockeys. Newspapers such as the *Morning Telegram* in New York were published, devoted exclusively to theatrical and sporting news. Never mind what was happening in Germany or Japan—the important news concerned who was riding whom.

But more specialized information was also needed by the bookies of America. Their customers wanted to know the results fast, wanted to collect their winnings fast so they could reinvest the money in the next race. Into being came wire services, companies, controlled by gamblers, that supplied race results and other pertinent information by Western Union telegraph to bookie joints across the country. It was just the ticket, agreed the bookies, but, unfortunately, there was no nation-wide network to depend upon. Competition existed. One bookie might get the results from Hazel Park but be unable to tell who won the fifth at Hialeah. It was downright frustrating.

And then came Moe Annenberg.

Born in East Prussia in 1877, Moses L. Annenberg was brought to Chicago in 1884 by his father, a junkyard dealer. Moe quit school at twelve to go to work, and by age eighteen he was on his way as a strong-arm goon for the Chicago *Examiner.* In the newspaper wars of that era, Annenberg proved his value. He rose to the top as circulation manager of all Hearst newspapers in the country. In that capacity, he employed an army of young hoods who later became major gangsters during Prohibition.

A family picture of Moses Annenberg, founder of the national wire service for bookies, with his young son Walter, nicknamed ''Annie'' at college.

Contact with the underworld made the rising executive familiar with the potential of the bookie industry. Moe moved first to control the various racing publications, and then he turned to the wire service.

Largest of the several services was Mont Tennes's General New Bureau in Chicago. Annenberg managed to buy forty-eight percent of the company's stock. A Chicago gambler, John Lynch, bought forty percent, and the rest was scattered among Tennes's relatives. Unable to get working control of the company, Annenberg formed the Nationwide News Service in 1934 and began driving General News out of business. Lynch fought back until, at last, the Chicago syndicate—with whom Annenberg was allied—put pressure on him to sell out cheap. Shortly thereafter, Annenberg's new outfit achieved a virtual monopoly on wire-service business. And business boomed. Soon Annenberg was supplying fifteen thousand individual bookie joints across the country. They paid almost seven million dollars a year for the service. And that was just the beginning. By 1936, the wire-service empire was divided into fourteen corporations controlling thirty-six branches and servicing bookies in 223 cities. The wall sheet business—bookie joints papered their walls with charts of each day's races at various tracks—was divided into five corporations and numerous partnerships. The publishing business, which included not only the *Daily Racing Form* but the Philadelphia *Inquirer* and other good and bad newspapers, needed twenty separate corporations. Magazine and newspaper distributorships were administered by sixteen corporations, and there were scores of others to take care of real estate, liquor stores, insurance companies, and the like.

Not even Annenberg knew how rich he was. But he knew how to be careful despite his wealth. One day in 1936 he wrote a letter to his son-in-law, Stanley Kahn, who had made a proposal Moe considered reckless. The letter made this point:

"We simply cannot have everything. Mussolini, when he started out to grab

Sheets and guides to "sure wins" in daily racing from newsstands around the country. Opposite page, the Annenberg father and son at their trial in 1932.

Ethiopia, had to very carefully consider what he might be plunging into but Mussolini had nothing to risk because Italy was on the bum and those who might have opposed his ambitions had by far and away much more to risk than Mussolini. Our position is similar to that of the English nation. We in the racing field own three-quarters of the globe and manage the balance. In other words, the few little nations that are left have to pay us tribute to continue. Now isn't that the most beautiful and most satisfactory position to be in which ought to satisfy even me?

"Have you ever stopped to figure our earnings and how that might be upset by a little mistake such as we are discussing?"

But despite Annenberg's warning of "a number of enemies with unusual ability that are eager for a chance to get even with us," there seemed no real problem on the horizon. Across America the betting parlor became semirespectable. Some, in cities having many wealthy tourists or retired gangsters, were luxurious indeed. The 633 Club in Newport, Kentucky, for instance, offered padded swivel chairs so the guest could turn easily to the wall boards. Pretty girls took bets and brought drinks. A buffet offered tasty snacks, and a cashier's cage operated as efficiently as if it were in a supermarket. Wall-to-wall carpeting soaked up the sound, and air conditioning kept the customer cool.

The invention of air conditioning ranks with that of the adding machine in the development of the bookie business. For a time in the thirties one could walk along Market Street in Louisville and hear race results issuing without interruption from bookie joint after bookie joint. This phenomenon disturbed some good citizens who wondered if the cops were deaf. Gambling, after all, was illegal outside the confines of Churchill Downs. So the cops suggested that the bookies move upstairs. That helped a little, but on hot summer days with all the windows open, the telltale sounds could still be heard. With the coming of air conditioning the windows were kept closed. Bingo! Instantly, the scandal was at an end, and everyone was proud of the police force for having at last closed up the pesky bookies.

Moses Annenberg in 1936 after pleading guilty to having evaded income taxes amounting to $1,217,296. Opposite page, a day at the Italian races in 1949 for deported former vice boss Lucky Luciano, left, wearing eyeglasses.

Meanwhile, of course, there were more bookies than ever, but—out of sight, out of mind. Exactly the same thing happened in other cities from coast to coast. You can still hear old-timers in those cities talk about the bad old days when you could walk along the street and never miss a race.

Annenberg was riding for a fall, however. His wealth attracted the Internal Revenue Service, and his bland arrogance annoyed Elmer Irey, head of the intelligence unit. Irey put his special agents to digging. It took years and some lucky breaks, but in the end Annenberg agreed to a tax judgment of eight million dollars. A judge refused to plea-bargain and sentenced Annenberg to prison.

A bad ending? Yes, when it is considered that the old man died shortly after his release. But his son, Walter Annenberg, was appointed ambasador to the court of St. James by President Richard M. Nixon, a man who liked to gamble. Whether Nixon knew the father compared his personal empire to that of the English nation is doubtful, but the appointment was ironic nevertheless. The younger Annenberg, himself indicted with his father in 1932, contributed much money to Nixon's campaign. All of which brings to mind a statement made when Moe bought the Philadelphia *Inquirer* in 1936. An investigation noted "that some interesting observations might be made regarding the extent to which the payments of bank loans growing out of the purchase of the Philadelphia *Inquirer* are dependent upon the continued operation of gambling establishments throughout the United States."

FEBRUARY
SURE HIT CHARTS
Lucky 7 Best
FOR
Race Mutuel "Totals"
FAST SUPER SPECIALS
The Gold Card
PRICE
50¢
Lucky
GREATEST VAL
7
Key Numbers - Daily Se
LEADS - PARLAYS - DO
FOR MONTH
FEBRUA

SURE HIT
579 966
949 534 725 567 206 488
68 45 12 08 36 41 30 16 48 79
THE NEXT TWELVE ISSUES OF THIS PUBLICATION ARE AVAILABLE BY MAILI
SEND TO: OAK SALES, P.O. BOX 88, MOUNT VERNON, NEW YORK
DEAR SIR: ENCLOSED FIND $7.00. Please send me Lucky 7 Best Monthly
envelope for 12 months starting with .... (signify month)

Sure wins, sure hits, everything to
"help" the numbers customer.

The conviction and imprisonment of Moses Annenberg did not disturb the even tenor of the gambling industry. Nationwide News Service went out of business on November 15, 1939, and on November 20, five days later, Continental Press was born to carry on the vital services. The Kefauver Committee investigated the changeover and reported in 1951:

"It is one of the amazing aspects of this whole story that without any break in the service, without any dislocation of the facilities used in the entire process of obtaining, legitimately or illegitimately, information from the race tracks and without any disruption in its distribution, one man stepped out of this complicated business and another man took it over without any formal transfer or without the passing of a single dollar."

Mickey McBride, another old "circulator" of the Hearst press, was the man who took over. He later claimed it was all his mother's idea. She told him, he said, "You ought to try to do something. It's no use getting all them fellows thrown out of a job."

Some trouble did develop later when the Chicago syndicate quit paying for the service and tried to form a rival company, Trans-American Publishing and News Service, Inc. and a "wire-service war" threatened.

Trans-American folded up after losing a lot of money in 1945 and 1946, and the Chicago syndicate began paying for the wire service again. The Kefauver Committee made good use of the incident, however, and managed to get new laws passed that eventually put Continental out of business and changed the way bookies did business.

One of the new laws was designed to put the bookie in a federal-state vise. It required him to buy a federal wagering tax stamp and list his business address. At intervals he was also supposed to report the volume of wagering business done and pay a ten percent tax on that. Of course, in listing his address and admitting his business volume, the poor bookie left himself open to prosecution on the state level, except in Nevada, of course, where gambling was

Ads placed in magazines devoted to gambling. One even includes a slide rule for more scientific bettors.

legal. If he didn't obey the federal law, the intelligence division of the Internal Revenue Service might get him. And they were the boys who "got" Al Capone and Frank Costello.

As usual, the bookie adjusted according to local conditions. In New York City, where there were thousands of bookies and only a score of federal agents, the federal law was largely ignored. In places like Newport, Kentucky, where the largest illegal gambling operations in the country were centered on a scale rivaling Las Vegas, and, of course, local police were corrupt, the bookies faithfully bought the tax stamps and paid the ten percent tax. They cheated a bit, of course, but at least they went through the motions.

Attorneys for some gamblers maintained loudly that if tested the law would be ruled unconstitutional since in effect, it forced a gambler to testify against himself. Yet no suit was filed for years. Government attorneys said privately that the legal eagles were probably right, and for that reason they advised the IRS and the Justice Department not to demand vigorous enforcement of the law. A sort of standoff existed for a decade or more, an unwritten agreement on both sides not to rock the boat.

It was a situation particularly frustrating for local reformers. To know that ample evidence against gamblers was available for the asking and yet to see their officials ignore the opportunity and even deny its existence was a continual challenge. But nothing much was done about it until 1961, when the citizens of Newport installed a special judge, got a special grand jury and a special state attorney, and went after the wagering tax records. On the basis of the evidence, literally scores of indictments were returned. Meekly, the gamblers pleaded guilty to lesser charges and paid fines.

Following the election of George Ratterman as sheriff in 1961, the classic squeeze was applied. Ratterman, a former football player for the Cleveland Browns in the days when the team was owned by Mickey McBride, vowed to clean up Newport and the surrounding county. The day came. Federal agents arrested every bookie operating without a wagering tax stamp, and Ratterman's deputies arrested everyone operating with the stamp. It was a clean sweep, a beautiful example of local-federal cooperation.

It was also the end of the wagering tax law as written. A test case was filed in another jurisdiction. Eventually, the U.S. Supreme Court ruled that the law was unconstitutional as drafted since it forced gamblers to testify against themselves. There was talk of a new law, tailored to meet the Supreme Court's objections, but nothing was done for years. President Kennedy was dead, the war on crime conducted by his brother Robert was slowly expiring, and the pendulum began swinging the other way. Soon there was increasing pressure on state and national levels to legalize gambling. The Nixon years, infected with cynicism and corruption, gave the drive momentum. So it was that when at last, in 1974, Congress did pass a new, revised wagering tax bill, it received almost no attention, and Internal Revenue Commissioner Donald Alexander was able to assign enforcement of the law to that small, overworked agency, the Alcohol and Tobacco Tax Bureau. This decision by Alexander, a Nixon appointee, meant that the law would be completely ineffective, but in the climate of the times no one protested.

The bookie business continued to blossom. Even the legalization of off-track betting in New York proved a blessing to the bookies. While the OTB offices were crowded and the state reported a nice take in taxes, the boys in the backroom were busier than ever. They offered credit, the cynics pointed out, and sometimes much better odds. Besides, a lot of people could now ask the age-old question: If it is morally and legally right to bet in an OTB office, why is it wrong to bet with one's friendly neighborhood bookie?

The inclination to bet was stronger than ever, since the New York metropolitan area was saturated with advertising for various forms of legal gambling such as lotteries. The author had the experience of participating on a radio talk-show sponsored, in part, by a legal gambling operation. Every time he would make a point about the evils of gambling, there would be a pause for a commercial about the thrill and profit of taking a chance. Obviously, instead of driving the bookie out of business, as proponents had predicted, the state had been forced to compete with him. And in the process, a lot of new gamblers were created, making sure the demand kept up with the supply.

Internal Revenue Commissioner Donald Alexander. At right, in the early 1900s, to bet on the horses in New York one went to a racetrack like Saratoga; today, it is simply a matter of visiting a handy Off-Track Betting office like this one on Broadway.

But this history of bookies wouldn't be complete without the saga of two betting commissioners.

Ed Curd was a Kentucky boy growing up in the bluegrass area of Lexington where thoroughbreds live like kings behind white fences. Everyone gambled in those happy days, and a man like Colonel Edward Bradley —gambler, horse breeder, and Kentucky Derby winner—was the *beau ideal* of many underprivileged youths.

The dream was reinforced when Curd, the young man from Cave City, opened a small handbook in Lexington. The cops quickly raided it. Curd took his problems to the elderly mayor, who proved to be a man of compassion and refinement. Years later, Curd liked to recall the mayor's words.

"'Son,' he said, 'since the beginning of time, since the days of Adam and Eve, man has done two things: he has fucked and he has gambled. It's jist human nature, son, and around here we don't try to discourage it. We jist want to make sure you don't knock up some little gal and that you pay your debts like a man should. Now, I like what I've heard about you, son; you've got the makings of a gentleman. You jist go back to work and fergit about this shit. I'll take care of everything.'"

The old man was as good as his word, and Curd became an accepted bookie and, eventually, a recognized handicapper. His views as to odds were widely sought by the sportsmen of the area. The Mayfair Bar became Curd's headquarters and it achieved a national reputation.

With everything going well, Curd began following the horses to Miami in the winter. Eventually he bought a large house half-covered with flowering hibiscus on Star Island in Biscayne Bay.

Colonel Edward R. Bradley made book at tracks in the Mississippi Valley in the 1880s and then obtained interests in gambling casinos in various parts of the country. At his Idle Hour Stock Farm in Kentucky, Bradley attempted to beat the odds against producing winning horses.

Trouble developed when the Kefauver Committee started poking around in 1950. Curd was identified as Frank Costello's bookie, proof if nothing else of how far the Kentucky boy had come in his chosen profession.

The IRS was impressed, and immediately began investigating. Curd was astonished, unbelieving. He was no criminal. Why, the best people of Lexington, of the country, bet with him! It was an outrage.

Insensitive to such nuances, the tax men secured indictments charging six counts of tax evasion. Curd sold his $400,000 bluegrass farm and fled to Canada. Eventually run out of there, he wandered around the Caribbean a year or two before deciding that the gentlemanly thing to do was to pay his debt—whether he believed he owed it or not. So late in 1958, he turned himself in at Detroit. Two days later in Lexington he pleaded guilty and was sentenced to six concurrent one-year terms. That wasn't too bad, but the almost $400,000 in taxes and penalties really hurt.

When Curd was released in September 1959, he realized he would be a marked man in Kentucky, so he returned to Nassau, where he found an atmosphere to his liking. The town was small, and the white population even smaller. With the coming of legal gambling on Paradise Island, the political climate was favorable, too. Curd settled down in a big house on the hill overlooking the harbor. It had wide porches, rocking chairs, and was next door to Government House where the royal governor lived.

By the time the Bahamas became independent, Curd had put his roots down. As of this writing he is reported to be in charge of plans for a new, government-owned casino planned at Cable Beach. He is, after all, an authority in the vital field of credit—he knows who the big players are and how much credit to allow them. Such knowledge is essential to a large casino just as it is to a successful bookie operation.

It would appear then that after years of wandering, Ed Curd has achieved his dream and become a Kentucky gentleman—in Nassau.

Ed Curd, the bookie from Kentucky who achieved a national reputation.

Attorney General Robert F. Kennedy waged a war against organized crime and racketeering in the 1960s.

The increasing volume of betting in this country has created a new type of bookie — the layoff bettor. Operators as successful as Ed Curd cannot afford to handle all the bets they receive on a popular race such as the Derby or a heavyweight championship fight so they "lay off" a portion of it with a man who specializes in such bets. In effect, he sells insurance, but to make a profit he must be a master at odds and percentages. Attorney General Robert F. Kennedy put it this way in testimony before a House committee in 1961:

"The layoff men at the top of the bookmaking organization are in daily contact with each other to reinsure bets and divide the action, thus assuring that all make a profit and no one takes an exorbitant risk.

"These people conduct their business by telephone. When local authorities get close to them, they merely pick up stakes and move to another jurisdiction. The best example of this moving to frustrate local police is the case of a man who started operations as a layoff man in the Midwest in 1946. He moved to another town in 1949 and to Newport, Ky., in 1950. In 1952, under pressure of the Kefauver investigations into

organized crime, he moved to Montreal, Canada. When the Royal Canadian Police raided his establishment, he moved back to Newport."

And, it might be added, when in the summer of 1961 Kennedy's war on crime put renewed pressure on this individual, he moved to Blair House, north of Miami Beach in Surfside.

His name was Gilbert Lee Beckley, and to his colleagues in organized gambling he was "the Brain." A pleasant, cheerful fellow, he tried to have a homelife like anyone else. But his marriage ended in divorce when his son developed a disability that made it difficult to read, let alone do simple mathematics.

Beckley flourished at the teamster-financed Blair House — Jimmy Hoffa had a pad there, too — until the author wrote a newspaper story about his activities. Inspired, the FBI paid the Brain a visit. A Negro agent dressed as a chauffeur was at the wheel of the big Cadillac that drove up to the apartment house one day. Two well-dressed FBI agents sat in the back, doing their best to look like bodyguards. The doorman was informed that the chauffeur wanted to deliver a case of Scotch to Mr. Beckley. He allowed the men to use the elevator, the chauffeur balancing the box on his shoulder as if it weighed a ton. In reality, it contained a search warrant and a walkie-talkie.

Beckley was accustomed to receiving expensive gifts. When he looked out through his one-way glass peephole and saw the box of liquor on the chauffeur's shoulder, he opened his door. The three agents rushed inside. Beckley, dressed casually in a Japanese robe—during World War II he had helped "liberate" a geisha house in Tokyo—tried to destroy his records but was prevented. The records were in code, but when broken they provided evidence of a multimillion-dollar illegal empire.

The indictments that resulted were, for Beckley, the beginning of the end. He fought back, but his troubles piled up as new indictments were returned in other cities. In an effort to win some friends, he became a consultant to the National Football League, allegedly advising on precautions to take to prevent games from being fixed. But his troubles mounted.

Sometime in 1972, Beckley vanished. Abruptly. Completely. Finally. He remains missing at the time of this writing, and there are indications that his disappearance will ultimately rank with that of the legendary Judge Crater.

Some law-enforcement officials maintain that Beckley is dead, murdered by the crime syndicate to keep him from breaking under the strain and talking too much. Or perhaps because he did talk too much to Commissioner Pete Rozelle's gumshoes. But that is the standard explanation when someone—be it Joe Bananas or Patty Hearst—drops out of sight.

Some others whisper that the Brain has gone to limbo. Where and what is limbo? Well, no one is quite sure, but it could be

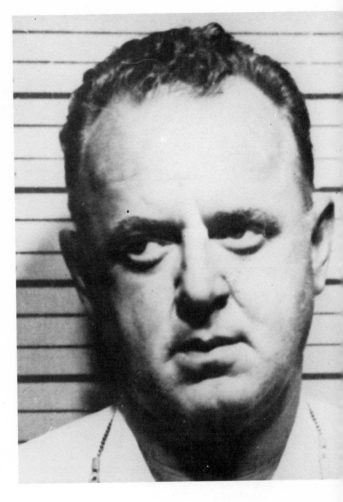

Gilbert Lee Beckley, "the Brain" who headed a multimillion-dollar illegal empire before mysteriously disappearing in 1972.

The one-mile trot being raced without spectators due to a strike by pari-mutuel workers at Roosevelt Raceway, Westbury, New York, in 1975. With the rise of OTB, horse racing may eventually come to this.

Eden, lost Atlantis, or some happy isle in the Caribbean where wealthy gangsters can relax and layoff bettors can put down their burdens.

If there isn't such a place, perhaps there should be.

Meanwhile, things continued without Beckley, and the shape of the future became visible at Roosevelt Raceway in Westbury, New York, on March 3, 1975.

Nine harness races were run on schedule and purses totaling $53,500 were paid. But there was no one in the stands to watch. No one at all.

The bets were all in—at the downtown offices of New York's Off-Track Betting parlors, and the parlors had closed before the races under the lights at Roosevelt began.

A strike of pari-mutuel ticket workers was responsible for the bizarre event. The track management closed the gates to patrons to avoid trouble—for who wants to watch a race if he can't bet on it?

The Off-Track Betting handle for the evening was $995,314, and spokesmen deplored the fact that racetrack patrons did not know the track would be closed in time to get their bets down off track.

But the absence of a crowd made every-

thing at the track more efficient. The races were run every seven minutes instead of every half hour, since there was no need to give suckers time to bet. The entire card was run by 9:14 P.M. instead of the usual 11 something o'clock.

Drivers noted that everyone was more relaxed, more "natural," but some felt it was "kind of dull" without a crowd booing or cheering.

But OTB officials, who had already won the right to accept bets on out-of-state races, said privately that the handwriting was on the wall. Given enough legal betting parlors, there would be no need to burn gasoline getting to a track. The time would come when all races would be run in silence, watched only by television cameras.

Indeed, some bookies looked ahead to an even greater day when the race itself would be obsolete. In lieu of it, betting officials would feed data about bloodlines and the records of sires into a computer and, before you could say, "Improve the breed," the winners would be known.

How do you "fix" a computer? Easy. You get this little electronic device they call a red box, see, and you hook it up to a shortwave transmitter like a walkie-talkie, see, and then you whistle into it just at the right time, see . . . .

ACKNOWLEDGMENTS

The authors would like to thank the following people for their help in research and preparation of material for this book: Mr. Michael Foley, for use of photographs he kindly loaned us on the Canfield House at Newport, Rhode Island. Mr. Foley lives in the former gardener's cottage of the former Canfield estate, and gave us a guided tour of Canfield House. Ms. Dewey, owner of Canfield House, for her kind permission to photograph the house from top to bottom. For aid in translation of foreign material, Jennifer Siebens, Hector Arroyo, Anthony Rosado, and Fred Arroyo. The staff, including Tayeb Jafferji, of the New York Public Library Reproduction Division. The staff of the Lincoln Center Library, Theater Collection; Leslie Goldblatt for aid in production; and Margo Hazel for collation of material important to this book.

PICTURE CREDITS

Authors' Collection
2, 3, 4, 5, 6, 8, 9, 10, 11, 39, 85, 86, 87, 88, 89, 96, 98, 99, 100, 101, 108, 109, 122, 128, 129, 132, 134, 136 B, 142, 143, 146, 158, 159, 160, 171, 172, 173, 174, 194, 198, 199, 201, 205

George S. Bolster Collection
80, 81

Columbia University
62, 63, 66, 67, 70, 71, 103, 104, 105, 106, 190, 191

Marshall A. Fey
163

New York City Police Museum
110, 179, 189

New York Public Library Picture Collection
12, 13, 14, 15, 16, 17, 18, 19, 20 21, 22, 23, 24, 25, 26, 27, 28, 29, 30, 31, 32, 33, 34, 36, 37, 38, 40, 42, 43, 44, 45, 46, 47, 48, 49, 50, 51, 52, 53, 54, 55, 56, 57, 58, 59, 60, 61, 64, 65, 68, 69, 70, 71, 72, 73, 76, 77, 78, 79, 82, 83, 84, 90, 91 R, 92, 94, 95, 97, 102, 107, 112, 113, 114, 115, 117, 118, 119, 120, 126 R, 127, 140, 141 L, 144, 145, 147, 151, 164, 165, 166, 167, 168, 178, 180, 181, 182, 183, 184, 185, 186, 187, 188, 192, 202

New York Public Library Theater Collection
74, 75, 91 T & L, 93, 124, 125, 130, 131 R

Swedish National Tourist Office
150 T

United Press International
116, 121, 123, 126 L, 131 T & B, 133, 135, 136 T, 137, 141 R, 148, 149, 150 B, 152, 153, 155, 156, 157, 162, 169, 170, 175, 176, 193, 195, 196, 197, 200, 203, 204

Wide World
206

INDEX